Transcending Time
with
Thomas Jefferson

Is the Constitution
Still Applicable Today?

Stephen D. Hanson

iUniverse, Inc.
New York Bloomington

Transcending Time with Thomas Jefferson

Is the Constitution Still Applicable Today?

Copyright © 2010 by Stephen D. Hanson

iUniverse books may be ordered through booksellers or by contacting:
iUniverse
1663 Liberty Drive
Bloomington, IN 47403
www.iuniverse.com
1-800-Authors (1-800-288-4677)

ISBN: 978-1-4502-4021-5 (pbk)
ISBN: 978-1-4502-4023-9 (ebk)
ISBN: 978-1-4502-4022-2 (hbk)

Library of Congress Control Number: 2010909680

Printed in the United States of America
iUniverse rev. date: 6/28/10

Contents

Introduction

I grew up in a small town in Minnesota, the fifth of eight children of Howard and Clara Hanson. My father was a self-employed businessman and also served as the mayor of the township for a number of years. We were brought up with a religious background and conservative values. You'd never know both of my parents voted for the democrat in every election that they participated in. Back then, I believe a democrat would be more conservative than the average republican of today. My parents believed in self choice and that life revolved around the family.

We lived close to our grandparents on both sides of the family, and some of my fondest memories include those people. I cannot remember a time that I was not proud of my family. We were always a very proud family.

My father was diagnosed with rheumatic fever as a child, which damaged his heart and left him with serious medical problems over the years. My mother was the rock of the family, raising all eight children and taking care of my father. She was always there to support dad personally and with his business ventures. Being in a small town, dad's business struggled since there was more competition than the town could support. Even with that, trying to support such a large family and his health issues, he never complained and continued working extremely long hours. He never asked for a handout or support from anyone, including the government. We were self-sufficient. Eventually dad had to close the store and take a job in another town, which made it difficult on us all.

I remember he confided in me one day. "Other than my family," he said, "what makes me proudest is that I can look every man in the eye as I have paid every debt I've ever incurred personally or through my business."

We were a very patriotic family, and growing up there was always talk of politics around the supper table. My brother Jon joined the Air Force, and my brother Bob and I both went to Vietnam. That experience brought me a deeper love for this nation. Contrary to news reports, the war taught me that America is a just and humane country. Even in war, we had rules we had to follow. While some abuses happened, just like in the civilian world, they were not tolerated. I was appalled at the news reports and movies depicting our soldiers as pot smoking, blood thirsty animals.

After leaving the service, I entered the financial world and worked in many states with varied positions. This opened my eyes to how different some states were from others. I didn't realize at the time that this was as our Founding Fathers intended it to be. I met a great many people and saw that this country offered a wealth of opportunities for those who had goals and a plan to achieve them. I also met many people who seemed willing to just get by—most often with a little help from the rest of us.

Ronald Reagan was the first President who inspired me. He talked about America's greatness. He said America was like a "Shining City on the Hill." He talked about how illustrious America is when government gets out of the way and lets the people do its work. He met challenges with a smile and humor and looked at all Americans as blessed people. He had the courage to stand up to the Soviet Union on moral grounds. He cut taxes and the economy soared. He was a true American icon.

I decided to write this book as politics and history have always been a huge part of my life. I have been an avid reader of history and have read books that include these titles: *Slouching Towards Gomorrah, Liberty and Tyranny, The Making of America, The 5000 Year Leap, Real Change, 1776, The Founding Brothers, Common Sense, American Sphinx: The Character of Thomas Jefferson, When Character Was King, America Alone, Peace War and Politics, Fleeced, The Life of George Washington, Ronald Reagan, Thomas Jefferson in His Own Words, The Autobiography of Benjamin Franklin, Polk Conspiracy, High Crimes and Misdemeanors, Winston Churchill,* and *The Real Thomas Jefferson* among others.

I mention these books because I highly recommend them to gain insight into how and why our country was founded. I believe that Thomas Jefferson and George Washington were two of the most important figures in our nation's history: President Washington with more strength and courage than any man I have ever read about and Jefferson with insight that is beyond remarkable. While James Madison was the primary author of the Constitution, he relied greatly upon Jefferson and his writings.

Another reason for my putting pen to paper is that in speaking to many people, I have found that they do not know how and why this country was formed or where the founders got their inspiration and foresight.

This book is written in a fictional interview format with Thomas Jefferson. I wrote this book in an interview format as I believed it would be enlightening and an easy way for readers to understand the issues we are facing. It is what I believe reflects the ideas of Thomas Jefferson then and what he would believe today. I have included numerous quotes from Thomas Jefferson, the Founding Fathers, and other historical figures to illustrate their beliefs and to support my interpretation of their goals for America. I am attempting to show that the issues that faced them are in many ways the same issues we are struggling with today. This is an attempt to demonstrate that the values that formed this great country are still true today. Many now presume that what the Founding Fathers believed then are no longer applicable today. That is the reason that the interview takes place simultaneously in the past and present. The causes for liberty remain and the reasons for its loss are constant.

In writing the Constitution, the Founding Fathers studied the history of other governments to see what led to their greatness and to their demise. They took great care in their writings to protect all citizens from government infringing on their liberty and freedoms. They worked through the Articles of Confederation with the thirteen colonies to form the foundation of the Constitution. Once the Articles of Confederation were accepted in principle, the Constitution was written. Some amendments had to be made to the Constitution in order to get all thirteen colonies to ratify it, thus we have the Bill of Rights. They are the first ten amendments to the Constitution. This was an almost impossible task, but they were able to accomplish it as they all had one clear and common goal: individual freedom.

It is very clear that Jefferson and the others were concerned with limiting what the government could do as the Bill of Rights is a restriction on the government. Many believe that they are too restrictive and that there should be more directives on what government rights and obligations are. Clearly, Jefferson believed that states should hold the majority of the power and that the federal government should not infringe on the rights of the individual states. The federal government should be limited in power and scope in order to protect all citizens.

Jefferson spoke eloquently about the dangers of the federal government being involved with banks and how he considered government involvement with the banks as the greatest threat to our country. I believe we are now at a crossroads in our country on this very issue. Will we have individual rights or drift into a state of dependency on the federal government? Will we unleash the power of individualism and capitalism or slip into the decay of socialism that has been repeated many times in the past? Jefferson stated, "The happiness and prosperity of our citizens is the only legitimate object of government."

Our ability to control government may be the greatest test of our future freedom. Will we accept the domination of government in our lives and hope that it will be just or will we return to what our Founding Fathers believed in: limited government with individual freedom, the right to choose our destiny, the right to succeed or fail on our own merits, the right to keep the rewards of our labors?

I believe we must return to our roots if we are to remain a great and humanitarian country—a country that has fought wars for the freedom of others yet not seizing the land or resources from those we defeated. We have sent our men and women into war for nothing more than the noble belief that everyone has the right to live free from tyranny.

Great nations have risen and fallen; almost all have crumbled because they lost their core values. Governments over time cease to remain moral, which is always the start of their collapse. Examples of this would be the Roman and Greek Empires and the old Soviet Union, Italy, and Germany. They usurp their citizens' rights and individual freedoms and, with that, corruption grows in the quest for power and control. Most times the citizens of those countries never see it coming because the governments are stealthy in their objectives. They deceive the people by promising riches and rewards to the masses for not being productive thereby taking from the few who are productive. It all sounds well, but soon the society collapses from the weight of itself. Which destiny will we choose?

1

About Thomas Jefferson

Thomas Jefferson was born on April 13, 1743, and died on July 4, 1826. He was the son of Peter and Jane Jefferson who were a distinguished family in Shadwell, Virginia. He inherited approximately 5,000 acres of land in Albemarle County, Virginia. Jefferson took pride in being called a hard-working man and preferred that to being thought of as an aristocrat. His father died when he was just fourteen years old and being the oldest son, he became head of the family.

He went to the College of William and Mary at the age of sixteen. He was known as an avid reader of books and most often studied until one or two in the morning, then rising with daybreak. He studied almost everything the college had to offer including agriculture, history, literature, religion, zoology, physics, mathematics, philosophy, botany, and anatomy.

He once said, "I had rather be shut up in a very modest cottage with my books, my family and a few old friends dining on simple bacon, and letting the world roll on as it liked, than to occupy the most splendid post, which any human power can give."

Jefferson loved to read books in their native language. Amazingly, he could read Latin, Greek, Italian, Spanish, and Anglo-Saxon. He learned these languages because he wanted to read of history in the original context rather than from a translated version. He was also an accomplished violinist and would regularly perform for dignitaries.

Jefferson was married to Martha Wayles Skelton, and together they had six children. Martha died ten years after they were wed, and he never did remarry.

Jefferson owned slaves throughout his life. While he did not believe in slavery, they were necessary to operate plantations in those days and to make it possible to compete in selling products. All plantations used slaves, and if you did not, your cost of operating would be so high that you could not compete and would fail commercially. Most of his slaves lived in Albemarle County plantations and Popular Forest Estate and another eighty lived at his Monticello estate.

When Jefferson was twenty-five years old, he was a member of the Virginia legislature and wrote a bill to make slavery illegal in the state of Virginia. The bill failed to pass. He freed seven slaves, five of whom were freed when he died as specified in his will. He believed that most would die or be killed if they were just set free. They did not have family ties to lean on for support or the education necessary to acquire the skill sets that would allow them to flourish in the free world. There were two slaves who ran, and Jefferson refused to pursue them. If they wished to have freedom, he felt, it was their choice to make.

On June 16, 1777, he wrote, in a bill to prevent the importation of slaves, "to prevent more effectually the practice of holding persons in slavery and importing them into this State Be it enacted by the General Assembly that all persons who shall be hereafter imported into the Commonwealth by Sea or by Land, shall from henceforth become free and absolutely exempted from all Slavery or Bondage."

In June 1785 he wrote, "Can the liberties of a nation be thought secure when we have removed their only firm basis, a conviction in the minds of the people that these liberties are of the gift of God? That they are not to be violated but with his wrath? Indeed, I tremble for my country when I reflect that God is just: that his justice cannot sleep forever: that considering numbers, nature and natural means only, a revolution of the wheel of fortune, an exchange of situation, is among possible events: that it may become probable by supernatural interference! The Almighty has no attribute which can take side with us in such a context ... I think a change already perceptible, since the organs of the present revolution. The spirit of the master is abating, that of the slave rising from the dust, his condition mollifying, the way I hope preparing, under the auspices of heaven, for the total emancipation, and that this is disposed, in the order of events, to be with the consent of the masters, rather than by their extirpation."

On July 14, 1787, he wrote to Edward Rutledge, "I congratulate you, my dear friend, on the law of your state (South Carolina) for suspending the importation of slaves, and for the glory you have justly acquired by endeavoring to prevent it for ever. This abomination must have an end, and there is a superior bench reserved in heaven for those who hasten it."

Ralph Waldo Emerson summed up slavery when he wrote, "If you put a chain around the neck of a slave, the other end fastens itself around your own."

Jefferson never did anything that would have prevented slaves from leaving his plantation. He often stated that slavery was the scourge of mankind and had to one day be abolished if this country would ever be able to live up to the ideals written into the Constitution.

Jefferson served in the Second Continental Congress in 1775. He left Congress that fall when his eighteen-month-old daughter died and his wife became very ill. He was the second youngest member of Congress.

Thomas Jefferson was the author of the Declaration of Independence. It took him seventeen days to compose the document. He had written eight principles that he thought crucial to the Declaration of Independence, which are the following:

1. Government should be based on obvious truths that no sane person would question.
2. That all people are ruled by natural law, the law of the Almighty!
3. Every person must be equal in the eyes of the judicial system regardless of his or her status in the community.

4. All rights are given to them by God and not by governments.
5. That man has the right to life and liberty and to pursue his life as he sees fit, that he has the right to obtain and keep his personal property.
6. Protecting the rights of the people is the government's responsibility.
7. Limits of governmental power are given by the people.
8. That when government does not protect the rights given by the Almighty, the people have the right to overthrow that government and form a new government that does protect those inalienable rights.

The Declaration of Independence is still considered one of the most important documents ever written.

Thomas Jefferson was the third President of the United States defeating the incumbent President John Adams. The election was decided by John Burr who cast the deciding vote. During his presidency, he was responsible for buying the Louisiana Purchase from France, which greatly expanded the country. He wanted to map uncharted land in the West and supported the Lewis and Clark expedition. Jefferson was always a strong proponent of remaining neutral in the war between Britain and France.

After his presidency, he founded the University of Virginia. His personal library was the foundation of the Library of Congress.

Jefferson believed in self-government—that free men have the right and are capable of making decisions that are best for them, their families, and the nation. He wrote, "We owe every other sacrifice to ourselves, to our federal brethren, and to the world at large to pursue with temper and perseverance the great experiment which shall prove that man is capable of living in society governing itself by laws self-imposed, and securing to its members the enjoyment of life, liberty, property, and peace; and further, to show that even when the government of its choice shall manifest a tendency to degeneracy, we are not at once to despair, but that the will and the watchfulness of its sounder parts will return its aberrations, recall it to original and legitimate principles, and restrain it within the rightful limits of self-government."

Jefferson's writings are some of the most voluminous in our nation's history, and he is arguably the most quoted political figure this country has known. Jefferson once wrote, "I am a real Christian, that is to say, a disciple of the doctrines of Jesus." I believe that sums up quite clearly the basis for his writings in the Declaration of Independence and the United States Constitution.

Thomas Jefferson died on the fiftieth anniversary of the signing of the Declaration of Independence, July 4, 1826. Coincidentally, John Adams, the second President of the United States, died the same day as Jefferson, only hours apart.

2

The Declaration of Independence: History's Most Important Document

I want to thank you for taking the time to do this interview with me, President Jefferson. I am looking for your views on what you wrote in the past and how you feel it is or isn't applicable in today's world.

Q: You are the author of the Declaration of Independence. What was your main goal in writing this document?

Jefferson: When reviewing history, in almost every case, individual rights and liberties have been limited by government. I believe these rights are given by God, not government. I was attempting to proclaim that all men have equal rights and since they are given by God, government cannot infringe upon these rights.

Governments historically have always restricted rights and this needed to be changed. Government must answer to the people. When it does not, the people must rise up and take back the government and put it back into the hands of the people. England was denying individual rights to the colonists and becoming more intrusive into everyone's lives through taxation and the court system. It was time to break free of their chains, and the Declaration of Independence was our official notice to the King of England of our intent to become a sovereign nation.

Q: What was the basis of your writings, what influenced you the most?

Jefferson: I looked back at history, as it is the only means to look to the future. There are two forms of government that are on the opposite ends of extremist. On one side you have government of tyranny, which occurs when a person or persons control all aspects of government and therefore the lives of the people under the government. On the opposite end of the spectrum you will find anarchy, which is the absence of law. This is just as bad for the people as tyranny. In the middle you will find law of the people—laws that control leaders and laws to protect people from each other.

Q: What specifically did you look at to come up with this conclusion?

Jefferson: First of all I looked at the Israelites. They divided the people into groups containing about ten families. Each of these groups had a leader. These groups of ten families formed larger groups of about fifty families, and there was an elected leader for each of these groups. This system continued up the spectrum until there was a final person who oversaw all of the groups.

Since the groups on the bottom elected their officials who in turn elected the officials above them, the people at the bottom had much control of their own destiny. Government was created from the bottom up rather than from the top down. Most problems were solved by the smallest groups not the government power at the top. History showed that the leaders would meet to discuss the problems of the society. This is a bottom-up form of government or commonly called people's government.

History also has revealed that when the leaders failed to follow the tenets, and power of the people was being usurped by its leaders, the nation of Israelites did not prosper. The people as a whole did prosper greatly when the principles of people's law were followed!

I also studied Anglo-Saxon culture. Their system of government was very close to that of the Israelites. They considered themselves free men and that all laws made had to be made with the consent of the people. In times of war they would grant additional powers to their leaders, but those powers were taken away again once peace returned. They were very freedom-orientated people who thrived with limited government. Their local leaders had more influence in their lives than that of the national leaders. They had laws that prevented their property from being taken from them or taxed without their consent. They had trials by a jury of their peers. Their general welfare laws allowed the injured citizen to seek damages from those citizens who violated his rights. They followed natural law, law that stated rights came from God and not from man, and that include women who had the same rights as men, which was not common during that period of time.

These were the two societies I studied most in trying to write the Declaration of Independence.

Q: Mr. Jefferson, you state that all men are created equal but yet you owned slaves. How do you explain that?

Jefferson: I believe slavery is the darkest period in our history including mine. In forming this nation, we had competing interests from the thirteen colonies. The union of these thirteen colonies was very fragile, and abolishing slavery would have doomed the formation of the country.

The northern colonies were in favor of abolishing slavery immediately, and the southern colonies would not have joined with the north if slavery were abolished because they felt it would ruin them financially. Most of us knew that when the opportunity arose, we would have to abolish slavery if we were to become a just nation. We needed all of the colonies to join the union if we were to survive economically and be strong enough to defend ourselves from other nations, especially England, France, and Spain.

Personally, I hated slavery but did not believe that most slaves had means or family support systems enabling them to be freed at that time. They had no wealth and, in many cases, very limited skills and were to face a hostile environment in which I did not believe most would survive. I had two slaves who ran away and I did not pursue them. The limited number who did try to flee my plantation I believe shows that I treated them better than what is typically thought of when speaking of slavery.

I considered slavery the biggest moral and legal hurdle facing this new nation. President Washington who also owned slaves felt the same way and echoed my beliefs. In 1778 I wrote a bill to prevent the further importation of slaves, which would eventually eradicate slavery for all time from this land. That bill was rejected.

Q: You originally wrote *life, liberty, and the pursuit of property* but changed property to *happiness*; why the change?

Jefferson: I do not believe you can have freedom if you do not have the right to acquire and keep property. If any entity is allowed to limit or confiscate your property, you will never have freedom. Historically, governments have always confiscated property for their own use and welfare. *Property* was changed to *happiness* because some colonies considered slaves property, and if we left it as property, we could see that we would never be able to abolish slavery.

In studying the Israelites and the Anglo-Saxons I saw that when people had the right to earn and keep their own property, all of society benefited. When government had the right to take or redistribute property, society collapsed. This was true with the Anglo-Saxons for when they elected a king who had immense powers, it was the beginning of the end for their culture. Alexander Hamilton wrote, "No man in his senses can hesitate in choosing to be free, rather than a slave."

Q: In the Declaration it states that if government becomes destructive, the people have the right to change it. Can you elaborate on this?

Jefferson: History tells us that through time government grows, not contracts. When it grows, it takes from its citizens to feed itself and gain power. Soon you have government controlling the lives of citizens when it should be citizens controlling government. If government becomes destructive to individual rights, then it is everyone's duty to change or abolish it. The ways to change a destructive government is, first, vote out of office those representatives who are not living up to their oath of protecting the Constitution. If that does not work, citizens must organize to create a movement in the country to make everyone aware of the issues facing them. Last, if there must be a rebellion, hopefully it will be a civil rebellion. A rebellion is necessary periodically to refresh freedom. The individual's right must always remain paramount. Margaret Mead wrote, "Never doubt that a small group of thoughtful citizens can change the world. Indeed, it is the only thing that ever has."

Q: You give a list of grievances with the King of England. Is this the control you were referring to?

Jefferson: Absolutely, the King of England was taking all rights from the colonies and its people. The taking of these rights was destructive to society and needed to be changed. This does not mean that action needs to be drastic, but when a leader's actions are deemed to be destructive to our individual or states rights, action must be taken.

Q: One of the grievances in the Declaration is this: "He [King] has made Judges dependent on his Will alone, for the tenure of their offices, and the amount and payment of their salaries." Please elaborate.

Jefferson: I once wrote, "The two enemies of the people are criminals and government, so let us tie the second down with chains of the Constitution so the second will not become the legalized version of the first." When judges are beholden to the King or to a government, no man can expect a fair trial. Judges must be responsible to the people. When the government has control of the judges' incomes and livelihood, the judges will carry out the wishes of their benefactors and not the law protecting the people. Judges are the last recourse people have to protect their rights, and judges must remain independent from government.

Q: Another passage reads, "He has affected to render the Military independent of and superior to the Civil power."

Jefferson: You cannot have freedom or liberty with an army that does not answer to the people. Any army must be controlled by civilians to monitor the army and the potential abuses of it. You also cannot have any federal army that is among the civilian populace and usurps the rights of the states. Armies of the federal government are designed to protect us from enemies outside our borders and never to enforce its will on the populace.

A great example of this is Hitler in Germany; he created his own federal police force, called the Gestapo, which answered to him alone. They had the power to enter your home, seize property, and imprison anyone, all without due process. Hitler never would have been able to have the power to murder millions of people without forming the Gestapo. What history has done somewhere can be repeated anywhere if we are not all vigilant.

Q: "For imposing taxes on us without our consent," you said. We are taxed now, many believe, without our consent, what are your thoughts?

Jefferson: Samuel Adams wrote, "If taxes are laid upon us without our having a legal representation where they are laid, we are reduced from the character of free subjects to the state of tributary slaves." You have elected officials who write and enforce tax legislation. It is your duty, your obligation, that when you feel that these are onerous or without your consent, to remove these officials from public office. It is within your power to make change. When the public becomes apathetic, the politicians gain power and curtail your liberties.

Q: You made the statement, "He [The King of England] has erected a multitude of New Offices, and sent hither swarms of Officers to harass our people, and eat out their substance." What does that mean?

Jefferson: Government must be restricted from harassing citizens to intimidate or punish them in order to take from them their personal property or gains. Government can be powerful and intimidating. The threats of arrests, lawsuits, audits, and other measures must never be allowed. A rule of law made by the people to protect its people must be followed. If left to its own, governments will become cruel and despotic. The desire for power is the seed that leads to the destruction of a free society.

Q: The government needs taxes so that it can operate to fulfill the services and needs of its people, but you seem to advocate restricting those powers of taxation. Why?

Jefferson: The needs of able-bodied people need to be fulfilled by themselves, not acquired by dependence on a government body. All governments try to fulfill needs as a way of increasing dependency on government. Governments are not magnanimous; in most cases they are a necessary evil that can be a wolf in sheep's clothing.

Look to your family, your neighbor, your church for help, not a central government. Individuals tend to turn to expedient or convenient solutions and often neglect to consider what recourses may be suffered long term. Politicians will offer you gold, but you must ask at what price will you have to pay for that gold?

There is always a cost to liberty when the government comes to you with a handout telling you that everything will be taken care of and your anxieties will be eliminated. Be guarded when dealing with politicians. Are they offering you something that will infringe on another's rights? If they are infringing on another person's rights and liberties, they will infringe on your rights and your liberties too at some point in time.

Q: Can you define for me what you mean by a "republic" that is referred to in the Declaration?

Jefferson: To define a republic I will refer to President Madison who offered the best definition that I know of: "We may define a republic to be ... a government derives all its powers directly or indirectly from the great body of the people, and is administered by persons holding their offices during pleasure for a limited period, or during good behavior. It is essential to such a government that it be derived from the great body of the society, not from an inconsiderable proportion or a favored class of it; otherwise a handful of tyrannical nobles, exercising their oppressions by a delegation of their powers, might aspire to the rank of republicans and claim for their government the honorable title of republic."

He spells out clearly that it is government of the people, by the people, and that government must abide by the majority, as long as those wants are Constitutional. People must be governed by laws laid down and not changed without the consent of those governed. The Constitutional Amendment process is the means to change the Constitution.

I appreciate your explanations of the Declaration of Independence. I would like to continue our conversation with your views on what you faced in the 1700s, what this country faces today, and how the Constitution is relevant.

3

The Bill of Rights: The Key to Affirmation of the Constitution

Q: Why was the Bill of Rights necessary? Didn't the Constitution cover everything that was needed as far as being law and a guide for our future?

Jefferson: The problem with the Constitution alone is that it did not spell out the unalienable rights given to us by the Almighty. Many of the Founding Fathers believe the Constitution by itself had a flaw by not spelling out these rights so that in future generations it could come into question exactly what these rights were. They also believed that they needed a vehicle in which changes could be made to the Constitution if the need arose in the future. They put a safeguard on how these changes could be made by making it difficult to change the Constitution—three-fourths of the states must ratify the change necessary.

The Bill of Rights was also necessary because they could never have gotten the Constitution passed by all the states without the Bill of Rights. George Washington, seeing that they could not get it passed, asked the states to submit recommendations to amend the Constitution. When the states came back, they had one hundred eight-nine recommendations. Congress whittled these down to twelve amendments and sent them back to the states for ratification.

Eventually the ten amendments were passed and became known as the Bill of Rights. I wrote on the passing of amendments the following, "The example of changing a constitution by assembling wise men of the state, instead of assembling armies, will be worth as much to the world as former examples we have given them. The Constitution is ... unquestionably the wisest ever yet presented to men."

Q: Was there much difficulty in passing the Bill of Rights and then being able to ratify the Constitution?

Jefferson: There was great difficulty with both. As I stated, Congress had to reduce the number of suggested amendments from one hundred eighty-nine to ten. That took a great deal of time and effort.

Once the amendments were agree to, the next chore before the states was to get all the states on board and ratify the Constitution, which included the Bill of Rights. Note that all future amendments that are passed become part of the Constitution. Delaware was the first state to adopt the Constitution, and four days later Pennsylvania signed on followed by New Jersey six days later. Approximately a month later Georgia and Connecticut approved it. It took over nine months for Massachusetts, Maryland, South Carolina, New Hampshire, New York, and North Carolina to ratify the Constitution. Rhode Island did not approve of the Constitution for three years and that only came after the rest of the states threatened to cut off all relations with the state including trade and defense.

You can readily see that it was no easy task to ratify the Constitution; many of the states ratifying it passed it by margins as low as two votes. With such low margins of passage, you can understand why it was impossible to try to make any major changes politically to the Constitution at that time as the process would have fallen apart and we would never have been able to form this great nation.

Many of us would have wanted to address the issue of slavery at this time, but we were unable as it was evident that there was no possible way we could have gotten the Constitution ratified if we had included the abolishing of slavery. It was important to get the states united and under one set of laws and then, at a time when it would be possible, address the immoral plague that haunted this country.

The goal of a moral and just government is to provide an environment in which people are free to choose their own destinies without fear of reprisal of a government as long as their decisions or acts do not trample on the rights of others. I wrote, "All authority belongs to the people."

Q: What do you feel is the most important addition to the Constitution that was made by the Bill of Rights?

Jefferson: Two things come readily to mind. First it spelled out the rights of all men clearly for all time. By spelling it out in such a manner, future politicians and judges would not be able to usurp the powers of the individual. While the Constitution spelled out the restrictions of government, it did not clearly define the rights of the individual.

Second, it began a process of remedies available to the will of the people to change the Constitution or add to it in the future, if events changed to where the people believed it should be amended. It states clearly the power of change lies with the people and not with politicians.

I wrote concerning this matter, "The firmness with which the people have withstood the late abuses of the press, the discernment they have manifested between truth and falsehood, show that they may safely be trusted to hear everything true and false, and to form a correct judgment between them." I also talked about the power of the people versus the power of government when I said, "I consider the people who constitute a society or nation as the source of all authority in that nation."

Q: Obviously if the Constitution was not ratified, the country would not be as it is today. What do you think would have been the immediate and long-term ramifications?

Jefferson: Immediately the results would have been disastrous. England, Spain, and France all had their eyes on this country. There would have been more wars fought, and in the end the country probably would have come under the control of one of these three countries. Even worse, it might have been conquered by two or more of these countries and divided up. For example, England might have controlled the Northeast, France the Southeast, and Spain the Gulf Coast states.

What that would mean to future citizens would be hard to predict. How would the World Wars outcome been different, advances in medicine and sciences, or in liberties around the word been changed? I believe the people of this country and the world today are better off because of the ratifying of the Constitution of the United States.

4

Three Separate Branches of Government: System of Checks and Balances

Q: The country was founded with three separate branches of government: executive, legislative, and judicial. How did this come to be?

Jefferson: We looked back in history and studied the writings of Polybius, a Greek who lived in Rome. He wrote extensively about having three separate powers of government. John Adams was the principal person who tried to form the government into the three branches. His ideas were not popular, but he persisted and eventually had the Commonwealth of Massachusetts adopt his principles. We owe a great debt to John Adams for being a visionary and steadfast in pushing forward those principles of checks and balances of the three branches.

George Washington wrote, "The Constitution is really, in its formation, a government of the people ... No government before introduced among mankind ever contained so many checks and such efficacious restraints to prevent it from degenerating into any species of oppression ... The balances arising from the distribution of the legislative, executive, and the judicial posers are the best that have ever been instituted."

We must always be diligent in keeping the powers of the government in check.

[A] Executive Branch

Q: Let's discuss the three branches starting with the executive branch. Tell me in your view of the power and limitations of this position.

Jefferson: The President of the United States is the individual leader of the United States. He is the Commander in Chief of the military forces, and he oversees all functions of the executive branch, proposes legislation for Congress to consider adopting, and is the chief ambassador for foreign affairs. The President has the right to veto any bill adopted by Congress where it takes a two-thirds majority of Congress to overturn a presidential veto. This is an important part of the balance of power.

Concerning the balance of power I wrote, "The concentrating [of powers] in the same hands is precisely the definition of despotic government. It will be no alleviation that these powers will be exercised by a plurality of hands, and not by a single vote."

The President is also the Commander in Chief of the military, thus having the military controlled by civilians. We envisioned the executive branch as being the weakest of the three branches of government.

Q: Let's try to break down each duty so we have an understanding of the responsibility. What do you mean by leader of the United States?

Jefferson: The President leads the nation with his vision for the country. He sets the tone for the country. The President reports to Congress at least annually and has the power to appoint federal judges with the advice and consent of Congress. He is the chief ambassador of this country in dealing with foreign nations.

Q: What are his responsibilities as Commander in Chief?

Jefferson: His first and foremost priority is to protect this country. As a civilian he oversees the military and makes all final decisions regarding war. It is his responsibility to maintain the forces and ensure they are adequate to the nation's self-protection. He does not have the power to declare war. In a declared war he will be able to use temporary authority as Commander in Chief. This is done so that decisions can be made in a timely basis and not get delayed through a legislative process. When the war is over, those powers are removed. The President as Commander in Chief keeps a check on the military from becoming too powerful.

Q: You state that he oversees the functioning of the executive branch. What does that entail?

Jefferson: Nothing more than being responsible that everyone employed in the executive branch completes his or her functions properly and that all of the actions of the staff are the President's responsibility. The President elected by the people serves a four-year term and is limited to two consecutive terms. His cabinet members serve at the pleasure of the President. Most cabinet members, however, must be approved by the Senate.

Q: Why is he the leader in proposing legislation to Congress?

Jefferson: You must have a leader, someone to guide Congress and this country in the direction that the people want. When an individual is elected, the people are telling the President and Congress what direction they want to take the country. That person, as long as those ideas are Constitutional, should try to carry out the mandate of the people.

The President carries a bully pulpit that allows him to speak more directly to the people than any other branch of government since he is recognized as the leader of the country. He has the right and duty to examine what Congress is doing and to speak to the public of their intentions, good or bad. This is a check on Congress to act responsibly and Constitutionally.

Q: What are his duties and responsibilities as leader in foreign affairs?

Jefferson: It would be impossible for any other country to deal with Congress, and nothing could ever be resolved dealing with such a large body of people. The President acts as a spokesperson for the country when dealing with foreign nations. The President cannot, however, enact any treaty into law; he must propose that treaty to Congress, which can ratify or deny the treaty. The presidential powers were intended by the Constitution to be limited in scope.

[A] Legislative Branch

Q: Could you briefly explain the purpose and the powers given to the legislative branch?

Jefferson: All laws governing the nation as a whole (federal laws) must be enacted by the legislative branch. No other person or body of government can enact laws. The President of the United States can veto any bill signed by Congress, and Congress can override a presidential veto with a two-thirds majority vote. That is part of the checks and balances of the three branches of government. The President must be moral and of strong character.

Abraham Lincoln said, "Nearly all men can stand adversity, but if you want to test a man's character, give him power."

Q: What is the responsibility of the House of Representatives?

Jefferson: All bills regarding government expenditures must originate in the House of Representatives. They are the larger of the two bodies, elected by districts within their state boundaries. The Representatives come from smaller areas of the states than the Senators, so they should be closer to the people they represent and should be able to more closely follow the will of the people. They have the responsibility to safeguard all the rights of its citizens.

The House of Representatives must approve by vote all bills enacted in either the House or the Senate. They serve two-year terms with no restrictions on the number of terms that they may serve. The purpose of the two-year term was so Representatives would not become career politicians. It was intended to allow more people from their own communities to serve. The two-year term also holds the Representatives more accountable as they must face the people in an election of their office frequently.

Q: And what are the responsibilities of the Senate?

Jefferson: Two Senators represent each state. Originally these Senators were elected by the individual state's Representatives. This was changed by the Seventeenth Amendment and, in my view, was changed in error as I believe it would be better if they were still elected by their state officials. The reason for this is that it would be easier to recall them if they were not protecting or looking out for the best interests of the state that they represent.

The Senate has the power to enact laws and approve spending bills originated in the House. They have the obligation to safeguard the rights of the country's citizens. Senators serve six-year terms with no limit on the number of terms that they may serve.

Q: The last branch is the judiciary. Can you explain its purpose?

Jefferson: The judiciary is responsible to see that all laws of the Constitution are followed and that all men are treated equally under the Constitution. They also have the responsibility to ensure that laws passed by Congress are Constitutional. The judicial branch cannot make law—that power is left solely with Congress. They interpret existing law to ensure justice is fair to all. They must not be swayed by public opinion or their own opinion. They must adhere to the law as it is written.

I wrote concerning this, "The majority, oppressing an individual, is guilty of a crime, abuses its strength, and by acting on the law of the strongest breaks up the foundations of society." I also wrote, "It is more dangerous that even a guilty person should be punished without the forms of law than that he should escape."

[A] General Discussion on the Three Branches of Government and Their Effect on Liberty

Q: What are your concerns regarding the powers of the presidency?

Jefferson: My fears back in the 1700s were well founded as the powers of the President have increased beyond the boundaries that were set up in the Constitution, and this is dangerous to society and its freedoms. The Presidents have expanded federal employment under their direction to millions of government employees, and it is growing at a faster rate than in the private sector. This makes more and more people dependent on the government and therefore reluctant to do anything to curb the powers of government. This at some point will lead to tyranny. Those salaries are paid by individuals' taxes, and eventually the government employees will outnumber the private workers and the system will collapse. Right now civil servants earn approximately 25 percent more than their private-sector counterparts. They enjoy more benefits than the private sector, and it is almost unheard of to be laid off or fired. These become jobs for life. With the amount of tax revenue needed to pay these wages and benefits and with the number growing, the day of reckoning is coming when revenues will no longer be able to continue paying these individuals.

I wrote, "A democracy is nothing more than mob rule, where fifty-one percent of the people may take away the rights of the other forty-nine." Trust me, that is government's plan as it feeds them the power over everyone's lives. Henry David Thoreau said it well, "That government is best which governs least."

Q: What are your thoughts concerning administrative law or presidential edicts?

Jefferson: This is truly dangerous to our society and future as a nation and blatantly unconstitutional. This amounts to the President writing and enacting law, which is prohibited by the Constitution. President Theodore Roosevelt was the first President to radically abuse this method of usurping the law to accomplish his goals. He believed he could act in any way that *he* believed was in the best interest of our nation. In his term as President he issued over a thousand edicts.

Presidents now can create new programs that affect the country without congressional approval. In the past these have included, for example, wage and price controls, trade agreements, aid for specific industries, and aid to certain groups of individuals. Congress shall make all laws and must be approved by the President. Not the other way around. Congress has been weak and inept in allowing the executive branch to steal their power from them. It must be reined in if we are to ever get the power of the people back into our country. We do not live in a dictatorship; we do not have kings who make laws as they see fit.

Q: What programs specifically do you feel threaten the country?

Jefferson: The President oversees national welfare programs, national unemployment payments, settles union disputes, Social Security payments, Medicare, and Medicaid. That is a massive amount of power to give to one man or one branch of government. It makes, in time, slaves of free men.

When you consider how many people have their jobs through government and are dependent upon government-controlled funds, you have a near majority of Americans who are beholden to the government.

Benjamin Franklin wrote, "He that is of the opinion money will do everything may well be suspected of doing everything for money." What I believe he is saying is that when a person controls money either earned or given, he should not be trusted. It is more power in one person or body than what is prudent in the long-term interest of this country.

Samuel Adams wrote concerning power given to any individual, "It is a very great mistake to imagine that the object of loyalty is the authority and interest of one individual man, however dignified by the applause or enriched by the success of popular actions."

The power of the presidency should and must be reined back to its original form. I also personally believe that if you are not moral, you are not fit to lead. We are now in an era where we look at whether the end justifies the means. This is a very dangerous thought process for our nation.

I also fear that people are not being informed on the issues that face them, and these are the consequences of not being educated. This leads to apathy. Regarding this I once said, "We in America do not have government by the majority. We have government by the majority who participate."

Q: Could you name some other areas that you believe that the executive branch has usurped the Constitution?

Jefferson: The government has gotten involved in making home loans and is dictating local education. In regard to banking I have never trusted banks, and I certainly do not trust a bank with government involvement. When the government got involved with banking, we have seen the end result—massive foreclosures and the loss of home values. Though I must admit the value of these homes was artificially inflated by the government to begin with.

In the area of education, schools no longer teach the basics that need to be taught for future generations to succeed. Why is it that the Amish community educates their students only to the eighth grade but yet their students score higher in test evaluations than students who graduate from twelve years of public education?

The federal government dictates what courses are taught and how they are taught. Shouldn't that be left to the local communities? Don't they know what and how they want their students taught? Shouldn't they be taught the influence that an Almighty Being had on the foundation of this country? When tax revenues that are earmarked for education are sent to the federal government, only twenty-six cents of the dollar is returned to the local community. How does that make sense? Locally, of the taxes that are earmarked for education, approximately 90 cents of each dollar, goes to education.

When students are taught such follies as global warming, political correctness, and how to use a condom, why are we surprised by the terrible results? When it costs an average of $12,000 to send a student to a private school but over $19,000 to send a student to public school, why do we still think the federal government is the answer? Why is it that teachers get tenure and then it is almost impossible to fire them regardless of their results in teaching our youth?

The only answers the government has to education problems are to spend more money. That clearly is not the answer! They do not have the vision or insight for change; change as always should be left up to the individual because individuals can effect the necessary changes. They spend money on home education, sports, and sex education—things that should be taught at home—yet question why education results are so poor.

I once stated, "Above all things I hope the education of the common people will be attended to, convinced that on their good sense we may rely with the most security for the preservation of a due degree in liberty."

We spend valuable school time on things that parents should be responsible for teaching, and it takes time away from reading, writing, mathematics, science, history, and study of government. As in almost all cases it is clear that government is not the answer.

I wrote: "If a Nation expects to be ignorant and free in a state of civilization, it expects what never was and never will be ... If we are to guard against ignorance and remain free, it is the responsibility of every American to be informed."

I would like to offer an example of not educating our children. Today you will see many people with a picture of Che Guevara on their shirts, caps, etc. He was a brutal person who believed in genocide. He was responsible for the murder of tens of thousands of people. He was a racist who believed that blacks were an inferior race and of no use to mankind. He believed his government should have final say over all free speech, religion, and even any form of entertainment. He admired Communism as the few should rule the masses that are too ignorant to have any say in how their lives should be lived. Now why do these people that glorify this despot not have a clue who the real person was?

Don't you think that people should be taught these things in history so that we don't make the same mistakes again? We don't educate people, we just pass them through. The answer to the education problem in this country lies in returning all education responsibilities to the states and eliminating the federal government from education entirely.

Q: Are there any other abuses you see to the Constitution?

Jefferson: I could make a list that would seem endless. They are involved in regulating manufacturing, energy, insurance companies, transportation, and, worst of all, licenses for communications.

Let us take energy first. People are not allowed nuclear power plants. Should that not be left up to the people to decide? It is cleaner and safer but the government's agenda's doesn't include nuclear power. Ask the question why. They tell you where and who can drill for oil and natural gas. Isn't that a state right? Doesn't that eliminate competition and increase prices? Doesn't that increase our risk to national security because we are dependent on other nations for energy?

Another area of concern is the establishment of the Environmental Protection Agency (EPA). When the bill forming the EPA was passed, Congress gave the President the power to oversee the EPA. Now without any checks or balances the President can regulate everything from our water systems to the air and our natural resources by using the EPA and usurping Congress and the individual states' rights. As an example, the President can stop power plants from being built even if an individual state needs or desires the power. He can cut off water that is used for irrigation of farms because he feels he wants to protect the habitat of an insect. Nowhere was it intended for one man to have that type of power over the states and of individual citizens.

Let me address regulating communications such as radio and television. Why do they have the right to say who may transmit and who does not? Is this not a product like every other product, a product that the consumer has the right to choose? Cannot a person turn on or off the radio or TV if he or she chooses not hear or see something? The government can dictate what can be said and what can't be. The government is now considering a fairness doctrine, which is nothing more than state control of the airwaves. Will you have choice with that in place? Will you have access to information or just information they wish you to have? It is a clear violation of freedom of speech.

The power of the executive branch far exceeds the limits set for it by the Constitution. It must be reined in. We [the founding fathers] were very concerned about the affairs of the people being placed in the hands of one person. We knew government is an inefficient entity that is incapable of handling problems timely and efficiently, and they invariably are fiscally irresponsible. I cannot for the life of me think of anything that the government is more efficient in and more prudent about in their spending than that of a privately owned business. They spend billions of dollars with little or no justification other than to buy votes and retain power.

Q: What are your thoughts on the House of Representatives?

Jefferson: When we were creating this government, and the separation of powers, we were intent of the power of rule to remain with the individual, the right to succeed or fail on his own merits. We did not want a government that insured success or failure.

Their primary purpose of the House of Representatives is to make law to protect the rights of the people. Representatives should always be looking out for the best interests of the people. These laws should be few.

James Madison wrote, "The powers delegated by the proposed constitution to the federal government are few and defined." I do not believe laws today are few.

Concerning government being involved in daily life I wrote, "The path we have to pursue is so quiet that we have nothing scarcely to propose. A noiseless course, not meddling with the affairs of others, unattractive of notice, is a mark that society is going on in happiness."

The House is in place to make sure the Senate does not pass laws that are not Constitutional and that the law will benefit society. The President must review the law and must sign off approving the new law.

Laws should be written so that all men of reasonable intelligence can understand them. On this I wrote, "Laws are made for men of ordinary understanding, and should therefore be construed by the ordinary rules of common sense. Their meaning is not to be sought for in metaphysical subtleties which make anything mean everything or nothing, at pleasure."

We did not want complex laws that would be written for the benefit of lawyers. Laws should be written in a form that the average citizen with an average education can understand.

James Madison wrote on this, which I quoted earlier. He also wrote, "The people are the only legitimate fountain of power, and it is from them that the constitutional charter under which the several branches of government hold their power, is derived."

As I stated earlier, all spending bills must originate in the House.

Q: Can you tell me a bit more about the purpose of the House of Representatives?

Jefferson: What we have is a republic, not a democracy. It would be impossible to function as a true democracy where everyone would vote on all legislation so that power is passed to elected representatives. I wrote concerning this, "Modern times have the signal advantage ... of having discovered the only device by which man's equal rights can be secured, to wit: government by the people, acting not in person but by representatives chosen by themselves, that is to say, by every man of ripe years and sane mind who either contributes by his purse or person to the support of his country." That is the manner in which every individual has a say in his country's future.

Q: Why do the Representatives have such a short term of only two years before facing re-election?

Jefferson: First of all it eliminates power as they face re-election often, so there is less inclination to vote against the wishes of the people of their districts. People have recourse to their Representatives in a short time frame if they go against the wishes of the majority of the people in their districts.

One problem that has been rising in the House is brought on by constantly redrawing the boundary lines for the districts. To illustrate this, an example would be this: within a state the district now includes two separate counties. The government decides to redraw the district by keeping the one county and taking parts of two other counties. They have been doing this so that they can include people who support their beliefs and eliminate those who oppose them. This is certainly an abuse of power and against the intent of the Constitution.

Each state receives Representatives based upon the population of the state with each state being guaranteed one Representative regardless of population. As the population grows, the Representatives will represent a larger population base. In 1929 it was passed in Congress that there will never be more than 435 congressional representatives in the House of Representatives.

Q: Doesn't representation based upon population give more power to the states with large populations versus states with limited population?

Jefferson: Yes and that is the reason that the Senate would consist of two senators from each state regardless of population therefore giving the smaller states an equal say in the body of Congress. While this is not perfect, it does protect large states from being ruled by smaller states and gives more say to large states as they contribute more to the nation as a whole when it comes to taxation and national defense.

Benjamin Franklin wrote concerning this, "The diversity of opinions turns on two points. If a proportional representation takes place, the small states contend that their liberties will be in danger. If an equality of votes is to be put in its place, the large states say their money will be in danger. When a broad table is to be made, and the edges of the planks do not fit, the artist takes a little from both and makes a good joint. In like manner, here, both sides must part from some of their demands in order that they may join in some accommodating proposition."

Q: What other responsibilities does the House have?

Jefferson: The House of Representatives can bring impeachment charges against the President, members of the executive branch, and federal judges. They bring the charges against the individual, but if the charges merit a trial as voted on by members of the House, then they are tried in the Senate. This is a very important part of the checks and balances of power. We did not want this to be partisan or used for frivolous issues. That is why we designed it so that one body of the Congress would make the charge and the other body, the Senate, would conduct the trial.

Q: What is the Senate's place in government?

Jefferson: Very similar to the House of Representatives except that they do not originate spending bills. The Senate was founded to look out for the rights of the states. They are responsible to approve bills that originated in the House just as the House is responsible for approving bills originated in the Senate. All bills approved by the two houses must have presidential approval. In case of a tie vote in the Senate, the Vice-President of the United States will cast the tie-breaking vote.

The states do have recourse to laws passed by Congress; they can under Article V of the Constitution nullify decisions made by Congress with two-thirds of the states voting to overturn the legislation and ratified by three-fourths of the states. The legislative and judiciary branches have no authority to overturn the states once the states overturn the legislation. This is an important part of checks and balances that was imposed to ensure freedom.

This right of the states has never been exercised by the states in the history of this nation, but I feel if the government continues to usurp the power of the people, it may only be a matter of time. This would be a nonviolent revolution! I do believe that, at some point, rebellion will be necessary.

Q: Why was it originally set up that the individual state legislatures would pick their Senators to represent them rather than by popular vote?

Jefferson: The Senators' purpose was to represent the states, not the individuals, as that was the function of the House. Since the passage of the Seventeenth Amendment, I believe the Senate is no more than another body of the House of Representatives.

We wanted Senators to look out for states' rights. Coming from state legislatures they would be more seasoned people than the

Representatives. Being elected by state legislators, they would be more inclined not to vote for anything that would weaken states' rights. They also would not vote for things that would not be in the best interest of their state regardless of national interests. We did not want them to think in national terms but in state terms.

States' rights have been repeatedly violated over the years, and I believe the Seventeenth Amendment is the principal reason why. William Davie, a delegate from North Carolina, wrote, "The senators represent the sovereignty of the states; they are directly chosen by the state legislatures, and no legislative act can be done without their concurrence." It also was to help keep the federal government from becoming totally dominant of the state governments.

I do not believe today's Senate looks out for the right of the states but are now national legislators.

Q: Could you expand on that premise of the Senate's obligation to protect the states?

Jefferson: The Senators are really ambassadors of the individual states to the federal government. James Madison wrote concerning federal government versus the states, "I may say, with truth, that there never was a more economical government in any age or country, nor which will require fewer hands, or give less influence ... From the chief officers to the lowest, we shall find the scale preponderating so much in favor of the states, that, while so many persons are attached to them, it will be impossible to turn the balance against them. There will be an irresistible bias towards the state governments."

James Wilson, a delegate from Pennsylvania, added his thoughts to those of James Madison, "A consolidated government that puts the thirteen United States into one, would not suit the people of America. The system before you, must stand or fall, as the state governments are secured or ruined."

Does that sound like the Founding Fathers wanted an all supreme federal government?

The Senate is charged with the responsibility of keeping the federal government from over reaching on their Constitutional powers and that includes insuring the executive branch powers are limited.

Q: When discussing the responsibilities of the House of Representatives, you stated that the Senate will hold trials on impeachment of the President, his executives, and federal judges. How is this done?

Jefferson: The House brings the charges against the officials, and if the House by popular vote believes that a trial is warranted, the matter is turned over to the Senate for trial with the Chief Justice of the Supreme Court presiding over the trial. The Founding Fathers wanted a separate body of government to try the case after another body brought forth the charges. This was another way of having checks and balances of power in our system. They felt that they wanted a body larger than that of the Supreme Court to try the case because with smaller bodies you are more likely to have prejudices that would affect the outcome.

Q: Let's move on to the judiciary. Can you tell me about their primary functions?

Jefferson: I wrote about justice years ago when I said, "When one undertakes to administer justice, it must be with an even hand, and by rule, what is done for one must be done for everyone in equal degree."

The main purpose of the judicial system is protecting our citizens from abuses. Judges are to make decisions based upon the Constitution. They are charged with reviewing laws made by Congress to ensure that they are Constitutional. All rulings made by the courts must be based on the U.S. Constitution and not based on any other country's law or international law. The courts are prohibited from making any law—that right is reserved for Congress alone.

I wrote, "I consider trial by jury as the only anchor yet devised by man, by which a government can be held to the principles of its constitution." I also wrote concerning justice, "Bear in mind this sacred principle, that thought the will of the majority is in all cases to prevail, that will to be rightful must be reasonable; that the minority possess their equal rights, which equal law must protect and to violate would be oppression."

Q: Where do you see our courts today in relation to following the Constitution?

Jefferson: The court has lost its way and needs to be brought back to its foundation. The court started to lose its way around the turn of the 1900s when Chief Justice Hughes stated, "We are under a Constitution, but the Constitution is what the judges say it is."

This is tyranny in its truest form, and the courts of today are following that same principle. They believe they can make law which is strictly forbidden by the Constitution. It is spelled out specifically they do not have the power to legislate. The Founding Fathers wanted continuity in the courts and not for them to be subject to being replaced by the whims of newly elected officials. This, however, has given them more power than intended. I wanted to have the court to have terms that they served to ensure they could be quickly replaced when they overstepped their powers.

There are measures to rein in courts that run amuck of their responsibilities. They are drastic measures. First, the country could have a Constitutional amendment that repeals the judges' lifetime appointments. The downfall is that judges might feel they are intimidated into making decisions to please the politicians and the populace in order to retain their position. The second option would come when it deemed that the court is so out of touch, or so corrupt, that its functions must be suspended. The government has the right to suspend the funding of the courts. This would make them non-functional. Judges would be forced to give up the bench and then would be replaced, hopefully, by more competent judges.

These are very extreme situations, but there are remedies in place to handle just those cases. It would take courage, but leadership and commitment always does.

Regarding justice I said, "Man was created for social intercourse, but social intercourse cannot be maintained without a sense of justice; then man must have been created with a sense of justice."

Q: Do you feel the courts of today do in fact try to make law?

Jefferson: Absolutely! You have probably heard of the term *The Constitution is a living, breathing document?* Many judges including some Supreme Court judges believe this. Politicians who feel retrained by the Constitution appoint judges that believe it is a living document. The Constitution was written very clearly to be a rigid document that could only be changed with a Constitutional amendment.

I wrote, "I repeat that I do not charge the judges with willful and ill-intentioned error, but, honest error must be arrested where its toleration leads to public ruin. As for the safety of society, we commit honest maniacs to bedlam, so judges should be withdrawn from their bench whose erroneous biases are leading us to fame or in fortune; but it saves the Republic, which is the first and supreme law."

Judges make decisions based upon other judges' past rulings. While precedent is important, they do not always look to see if those rulings were indeed Constitutional. Attorneys present these rulings to the court and the judges are not questioning whether that prior decision met the Constitutional threshold. They have a moral and legal obligation to look at the past ruling to see if they believe it was the right decision, Constitutionally. If they do not do this and most judges do not, they will continue the mistakes of the past rulings. Why would we use the precedent of bad decisions to rule on a case before the court today? Do you feel that will protect your individual rights?

I wrote on the matter of judges making law, "We have seen too, that, contrary to all correct example, they are in the habit of going out of the question, before them to throw an anchor ahead and grapple further hold for the future advance of power. They are then, in fact, the corps of sappers and miners steadily working to undermine the independent rights of the states, and to consolidate all power in the hands of that government in which they have so important a freehold estate."

If you do not have a set rule of law, you have nothing, and eventually you will have neither liberty nor freedom. Regarding the following of the Constitution, President Lincoln wrote, "We, the people are the rightful master of both congress and the courts, not to overthrow the Constitution, but to overthrow men who pervert the Constitution." Judges are not to be involved in the debate of the subject; they should be free of all biases and only be concerned on the Constitutional question before them.

Alexander Hamilton wrote, "The judiciary ... has no influence over either the sword or the purse; no direction either of the strength of the wealth of society, and can take no active resolution whatever. It may truly be said to have neither force nor will."

Q: What are the strengths of the jury system?

Jefferson: The jury system was designed so that a person accused of a crime would be judged by his peers, by people of his community who would be aware of local circumstances. This was done under Anglo-Saxon law. It was also devised to have a check and balance on the court system. If you did not have juries, you could have judges ruling on the accused that have biases.

The jury of his peers should be much more objective in their findings than a single arbitrary figure. There was a time when the jury would determine if the charges against an individual were Constitutional. A jury could decide against a judge's direction and determine that the crime was not just and therefore set the person free. This was another means that we used to try to control government and keep the power with the people. I believe that should still be the case today.

There must be a glaring miscarriage of justice for a superior court to overturn a jury's decision. I wrote concerning juries, "It is left, therefore, to the juries; if they think the permanent judges are under any bias whatever in any cause, to take on them to judge the law as well as the fact. They never exercise this power but when they suspect partiality in the judges, and by the exercise of this power they have been the firmest bulwarks of English liberty."

5

Freedom of Religion: How the Founders Separated God from Religion

Q: I'd like to start this off with one of the most controversial issues facing this country: God-given rights and freedom of religion. You stated in the Declaration of Independence, "We hold these truths to be self-evident, that all men are created equal, that they are endowed by their Creator with certain unalienable Rights that among these are Life, Liberty and the pursuit of Happiness." Why did you state that rights came from their Creator rather than from government?

Jefferson: I looked at the histories of past and present governments, and it was readily apparent that governments grow, and as they grow they take away the rights of individuals. This was true in the Greek and Roman eras as well as present day France and England. These governments became brutal and repressive to the citizens. Governments always promise more to the population in order to stay in power; to give more they must take more; this is most commonly done under the guise of being benevolent. Governments have no power without money and to get money they must take it from its citizens. Make no mistake about it, governments are not benevolent.

Rights from God, not government, can never be taken away. What man gives you, he can take from you! What God has given you, no man can ever take from you! It was very obvious to me that it must be clearly stated that government cannot give you rights. We wanted to create a new country where men are free and where the government answers to the people rather than the people answering to the government.

In creating the Constitution we believed in the guidance of God as Alexander Hamilton pointed out when he said, "For my part, I sincerely esteem it [the Constitution] a system which without the finger of God, never could have been suggested and agreed upon by such diversity of interests."

Q: What about those who state that this is not freedom of religion, but rather it is promoting religion?

Jefferson: God is the Creator—not a specific religion. Whether individuals have faith in God or not, it is their choice. The government shall not promote or mandate a religion nor mandate belief in a Creator. We took a great deal of time in developing symbols and statements for our currency. This was not done without great concern for every detail of our currency. We put "In God We Trust" on the currency to state clearly that we put our faith and trust in God for our rights and not in any manmade form of government.

We were not endorsing any religion as individual religions can be as nefarious as governments. We wanted something that all people use every day that would be a constant reminder that all rights and liberties were given to them by God and not by any government or king.

Look at the back of the dollar bill. You will see the pyramid. There are thirteen tiers in the pyramid, one for each original colony. The top of the pyramid is not finished; this represents that we knew the country would continue to grow. The right side of the pyramid is shaded, which represents that the sun has not risen over the land that has not yet become part of this union. Above the pyramid is an eye that oversees the pyramid. This is the eye of the Almighty, overseeing our nation and protecting its natural law.

Benjamin Franklin wrote, "God governs in the affairs of man. And if a sparrow cannot fall to the ground without his notice, is it possible that an empire can rise without his aid?" We have been assured in the Sacred Writings that except the Lord build the house, they labor in vain that build it. I firmly believe this. I also believe that, without His concurring aid, we shall succeed in the political building no better than the builders of Babel.

You cannot have a moral country without following the basic belief that we answer to a higher power. That higher power must be God and not government, which is another way of saying that man will determine what is moral and what is not. Without morals coming from God, ethics will change over time to make it convenient for those in power to remove those morals.

As George Washington said, "It is impossible to rightly govern a nation without God and the Bible." John Adams stated," We have no government armed in power capable of contending with human passions unbridled by morality and religion. Our Constitution was made only for a religious and moral people. It is wholly inadequate for the government of any other."

Q: With that quote aren't you saying you are promoting Christianity?

Jefferson: Not at all, Washington believed the Bible to be a book of virtue that should guide us in living our lives and with governing our nation. The Bible can be generic; it can come under many names. It is a guide for morality. That is far different from a government-endorsed or government-sponsored church.

James Madison wrote, "In no instances have ... the churches been guardians of the liberties of the people." Churches can become like government, in search of power and control over their members' lives. We have seen this in Europe where the churches and government became entwined and the people feared both equally. The Bible teaches virtues. Churches may or may not be virtuous, but in no case can they be allowed to increase their power by being in bed with government.

Q: Over time people have come to believe God and religion are one and the same and they are attempting to remove any reference of God in our society. Why could this be harmful?

Jefferson: If you review the constitutions of each of the fifty states, you will see that every one of them references God and that the rights of its citizens are derived from God, not from the state. States have been added to the union through time, and they have all felt the need to reference the Creator.

Washington wrote, "I am sure there never was a people, who had more reason to acknowledge a Divine interposition in their affairs, than those of the United States; and I should be pained to believe that they have forgotten that agency, which was so often manifested during our Revolution, or that they failed to consider the omnipotence of that God who is alone able to protect them."

I say, be aware of those who want to muddy the water, be aware of their motives. In writing the Declaration of Independence and when we wrote the Constitution, we knew that government would want to usurp the rights of its citizens. To accomplish this they must remove God as the benefactor of your rights. As long as rights are given by God, government will be powerless in eradicating your individual God-given rights.

Abraham Lincoln is regarded as one our finest Presidents. In his second inaugural address, he referenced God fourteen times and quoted from the Bible twice. James Madison stated, "We've staked our future on our ability to follow the Ten Commandments with all of our heart."

Q: You say that with the absence of God, the country will fundamentally change, why do you say that?

Jefferson: You have to have glue that bonds the country and gives it a compass to follow. Since 1963 when the Supreme

Court took prayer out of schools and Congress as well, we have seen a decline in the moral fabric of the country. In 1776, the Continental Congress was meeting to determine the direction of the country. We had Catholics, Protestants, Quakers, etc., but all agreed that prayer was necessary to bond us together if we were going to set aside our personal preferences for the good of the country. We agreed that it was better to have a prayer each day, even if the prayer wasn't from our own personal faith, than no prayer at all.

I believe that now with the absence of prayer it is much more of a divided body with self-interest over that of the country. President Washington said it best when he said, "It is impossible to rightly govern a nation without God and the bible."

Another example is the family. Since the 1960s births out of wedlock have sky- rocketed. The family does not revolve around God to keep it together and on a moral footing. Divorce has increased and violence is increasing because, without the family unit, children are left to form their own values from peers rather than parents. They cannot get any moral direction from the schools since prayer has been eliminated. Even a moment of silence for individual choice of prayer is not allowed. God is not taught in public schools even though it was the most instrumental factor in the founding of the United States. Without God and natural law as the foundation of the country being taught, the true basis of freedom and liberty will not be understood.

The government and thus public schools have expanded the concept of God and freedom to a concept of freedom from God and religion. The intent in the Constitution is clear, it is freedom *of* religion, not freedom *from* religion.. The results are higher dropout rates, higher violence in schools on top of the students not being taught the true founding of this country. I cannot think of any benefit to us as a people by the forcing of God out of our lives.

Q: Can you give me an example of government denying rights given by God to impose their will?

Jefferson: Abortion. With God giving every person the right to life, they must deny God in order to allow the state the ability to sanction the end of life. Man can justify all actions if they deny the existence of God and therefore rights bestowed on them by Him.

I once wrote, "My views on Christianity are the result of a life & reflection, and very different from that anti-Christian system imputed to me by those who know nothing of my opinions. To the corruptions of Christianity I am indeed opposed; but not to the genuine precepts of Jesus himself. I am a Christian, in the only sense he wished any one to be; sincerely attached to his doctrines, in the preference to all others; ascribing to himself every human excellence; & believing he never claimed any other."

Why would God give the gift of life to an individual and give another individual the right to extinguish it? Many say it is not life until it the baby is delivered from its womb. Science clearly defines that DNA is life, and that DNA is melded at the time of conception from the male and female. DNA is life as defined by science. The Constitution is intended to protect all life. Man had to deny that the rights of the individual came from God in order to allow the violation of the basic right to life that is afforded all men. President Reagan once said, "If we ever forget that we are One Nation Under God, then we will be a nation gone under."

Q: Rowe vs. Wade made abortion legal. What in your opinion is wrong with the law?

Jefferson: God created nature and that is the premise of natural law. Man cannot change natural law as they are made by the Creator. This nation was founded on the premise that it could be a beacon of light to the rest of the world. To set an example that a nation could live under natural law and its citizens would enjoy liberty and reject the tyranny that comes when government legislates laws against the natural laws of nature.

Ronald Reagan said it best when he proclaimed, "Without God, democracy will not and cannot endure." You can also look to John Adams who said; "You have rights antecedent to all earthly governments: rights that cannot be repealed or restrained by human laws; rights derived from the Great Legislator of the universe." If you believe in natural law, law that you are conceived with, then there can be no argument regarding abortion.

Q: One of the main premises of the Constitution is that all men are created equal. How does that relate to natural law and the existence of God?

Jefferson: In our readings and discussions it is self-evident that God created all men equal in his eyes even though they may have different tastes, ambitions, looks, intelligence, etc. If not equal under the natural laws, men could create a system that does not allow each individual to reach his or her own goals in life. Laws can be made to restrain them from self-fulfillment.

Under natural law everyone must be treated fairly. This is to include his life, fairness in judgment of him socially as well as judiciously. He cannot be treated differently for any reason to include social status or personal traits. Equal justice comes from natural law. Man will never have complete total justice if natural law is not followed.

The three branches of government outlined in the Constitution are the judicial, legislative, and the executive. At the Constitutional Convention of 1787, James Madison proposed the plan to divide the central government into these three branches. He discovered this model of government from the Perfect Governor, as he read Isaiah 33:22, as follows:

For the LORD is our judge,
the LORD is our law giver,
The LORD is our king;
He will save us.

As you know, James Madison was one of the principal architects of the Constitution.

Q: Can you give me some examples of rights that would be insured because of natural law?

Jefferson: Absolutely! Freedom of religion, freedom of speech, the right to own property including personal wealth, to work to provide for your family, to become educated, to be judged fairly by your peers as any other man would be judged, to choose your government, to protect yourself and your family, the right to privacy, the right to have your own conscience and the right to pursue happiness as you choose.

Q: How is the right to property covered under natural law?

Jefferson: The Creator allows man to work and keep the fruits of his labor which includes property. Manmade law can eliminate or reduce this right and would make it impossible to be just with every individual. Throughout history, governments gain power through the confiscation of wealth that was earned and rightly owned by others. The Creator gives each of us unique skills. Each man has the natural right to use those skills for his personal gain.

Q: What about being educated?

Jefferson: You cannot have a country run by its people without an educated populace. When you have an uneducated populace, you will be ruled by nobles, tyrants, and dictators.

Everyone has the natural right to pursue their dreams. If you don't have equal access to education, then those dreams and goals become unattainable. Natural law then would be violated. God is written about and discussed all through the process of forming this country, in establishing a republic where all men have an opportunity for life, happiness, success, and failure.

God was the premise of the Constitution. Why are the schools not teaching in history the role God had in forming this union?

They say mentioning God would violate the separation of church and state. That is pure nonsense. First of all God is not religion but even if it were, for argument's sake, it is important to understand how and why this country was founded. Are we afraid of educating our youth? It is extremely important to understand how ideas were created, the purpose of the ideas if we are to remain a free country that espouses freedom and liberty. To ignore history is to commit yourself to the same failures that happened in the past.

Epictetus wrote, "Only the educated are free." In regard to education look at Provision 215 article 3 of the First Amendment, where it states; "Religion, morality and knowledge, being necessary to good government and happiness of mankind, schools and the means of education shall forever be encouraged."

Q: Why can't governments provide equal rights?

Jefferson: If all men were saints, there would be no need for any government. With flawed men, there will be flaws in the distribution of rights. With rights coming from the Creator, all men will be truly equal, it is then up to the government to protect those God-given rights and not to interpret them.

One common misunderstanding is government's role. Government is assigned with the responsibility of protecting the natural law and not providing equal things to all men. By that I mean, each man has the right to keep the fruit of his labors and government cannot take his fruits and distribute them to others to make all men equally wealthy. It is in each man's soul to make the decision how to share his wealth for the common good of his community, it is not the government's right.

As I said earlier, natural law states that every man must have equal access to education and justice, which would allow them to reach the level of success that they desire. That is far different from the government providing success without toil at the expense of others. That would violate the individual, who has reaped fruits, his natural rights.

Q: What else would you like to add regarding God being a part of the Constitution?

Jefferson: When writing the Constitution, it took a tremendous amount of effort by all the framers. We came from very diverse backgrounds. Some were university educated, some had limited schooling, and others were self-taught. We were farmers, educators, politicians, military officers, lawmakers, and entrepreneurs. The one thing we all had in common is that we were very well read and had either seen or read how governments can become oppressive. This is not always done intentionally; it develops over time, in many cases so slowly that most do not see it coming. It often comes masked in being benevolent. Governments are not and will never be benevolent. To give to one they must infringe on others' rights.

Governments will change with the times to appease one group over another. Morals will change and be justified for reasons of the moment. Natural law will not and cannot change. If natural law is followed, all men will have their rights guaranteed and protected. Reasons for eliminating natural laws will be like masking a wolf in sheep's clothing.

I once stated and still believe, "God, who gave us life, gave us liberty. And can the liberties of a nation be thought secure if we have removed their only firm basis: a conviction in the minds of men that these liberties are the gift of God? That they are not violated, but with His wrath?" Indeed, I tremble for my country when I reflect that God is just; that His justice cannot sleep forever."

Q: For many years there has been debate over God in public schools. Where do you stand on this issue?

Jefferson: The issue always comes down to this: is God the same as religion? When we framed the Constitution, we were clear that the government shall make no law promoting or requiring any religion in society. Religion is man's individual way of choosing how to worship God. God being the foundation for our society is entirely separate from advocating a religion. It is imperative that our students learn the basics and principles behind our founding the country on God. It does not require that a person even believe in God, but that he understands the principles of God and natural law and how it applies to society as a whole. They need to understand how it guarantees justice and freedom for every person.

Many theories are taught in school. Many of these theories including evolution are not proven facts but are used to expand the students' ability to reason and make their own decisions by exposing them to ideas that they might not have addressed on their own. The acknowledgment of God, not religion, is essential for them to protect their rights in the future. If God was not important, then why did all fifty states ratify that belief in their own state constitutions?

God's role in the formation of the United States of America is a vital part of this country's formation and must be taught. It can and should be done without forcing any individual to acknowledge any specific God or religion.

Q: There are always questions whether this is a religious country or not.

Jefferson: I don't believe most Americans are religious in the true sense of the word, but overwhelmingly the country believes in God, and they believe the country should be a moral country. Average people do not have the time or inclination to consider ramifications of long-term decisions, but they do believe that God will serve in keeping America moral and just.

Imagine what this country would look like without any premise of God. Regimes without the premise of God do not have justice for their citizens. The Soviet Union, Hitler's Germany, and North Korea just to name a few. Without God there is no fear of death and consequence! By that I mean, without God, why be moral or just to yourself or others if there are no consequences brought to bear by God?

George Washington wrote, "The propitious smiles of Heaven can never be expected on a nation that disregards the eternal rules of order and right which Heaven itself has ordained."

Q: What about Sharia law? Isn't that a law based upon their belief in God? (Sharia law allows for punishment without due process and does not provide equality for women.)

Jefferson: When we were founding this country, we based it upon natural law as defined by Judeo-Christian values. Sharia law does not allow all people to have equal justice under our Constitution. You cannot entertain or acknowledge any beliefs or system that does not guarantee that all people be treated equally under the law.

The following I believe summarizes my beliefs then and now when I wrote, "I am really mortified to be told that, in the United States of America, a fact like this can become a subject of inquiry, and of criminal inquiry too, as an offense against religion; that a question about the sale of a book can be carried before the civil magistrate. Is this then our freedom of religion? And are we to have a censor whose imprimatur shall say what books will be sold, and what we may buy? And who is thus to dogmatize religious opinions for our citizens? Whose foot is to be the measure to which ours are all to be cut or stretched? Is a priest to be our inquisitor, or shall a layman, simple as us, set them, and to assume the blessings and security of self-government. That form, which we have substituted, restores the free right to the unbounded exercise of reason and freedom of opinion. All eyes are opened, or opening, to the rights of men."

Q: You are saying that the Bible is the path that will lead this nation but isn't that religion?

Jefferson: The government cannot impose any religion on its citizens. That does mean that the Bible cannot be or should not be a guiding hand in the moral direction of this country. The Ten Commandments deals with man's responsibility to himself and the treatment of others. What moral person would denounce the principle of the Ten Commandments?

George Washington wrote, "It is impossible to rightly govern a nation without God and the Bible." We would never tolerate a government imposing religion or God on any citizen of the country, but that does not mean in any way that the foundation of liberty does not come from the principles of God, which brings us back to natural law.

While there have been injustices in the past, hasn't the concept of natural law guided us on a more moral and just path than almost any government ever created in history? Do we not endeavor to protect every person's rights to almost a fault? Are we not the most tolerant country?

John Adams also wrote, "You have rights antecedent of most governments; rights that cannot be repealed or restrained by human laws; rights derived from the Great Legislator of the universe." My question to you is this: would you believe that you and your families are and will be better off with liberties given by God or given to you by man?

6

Second Amendment: Why the Founders Viewed Guns as Essential to Freedom

Q: One of the most controversial issues in society today is the issue of guns. The right to bear arms is the Second Amendment. Why do you believe in the people having the right to own firearms?

Jefferson: This is one of the most important rights of citizens if not the most important right because if you cannot defend yourself, you have no rights. You have to look back at history to understand the importance of the populace being armed.

Ancient Egypt, Greece, and the Roman Empire all had laws preventing their citizens from bearing arms, and they were at the mercy of their governments. That was fine while the governments were looking out for the citizens but brutal when they were not.

In more modern times, look at Stalin, who murdered thirty million people. Mao Tse Tung murdered over sixty million people. Hitler with his ethnic cleansing murdered twenty-one million people.

Rwanda murdered tens of thousands with machetes. All those people were at the mercy of their governments because they were unarmed and defenseless. People like to believe that brutality like this could never happen in the United States, but history tells us that it could if we don't protect our basic rights.

George Washington said it best when he said, "Firearms are second only to the Constitution in importance; they are the people's liberty's teeth.

Q: But many believe in the United States we don't need protection from the government.

Jefferson: That is foolish, making the assumption that this country will never have corrupt or evil people who seek power or seek to change the country fundamentally. What keeps a potential evil or an agent of change from being able to carry out their plans is that they cannot control the populace.

I once wrote, "Those that would hammer their guns into plows will plow for those who do not." Evil does not stop at anyone's border and hopefully they would see the danger they would face with armed citizens. Robert Heinlein wrote, "When only cops have guns, it's called a 'police state.'" If you want another view of history, look at the thoughts of Mahatma Gandhi, "Among the many misdeeds of the British rule in India, history will look upon the act of depriving a whole nation of arms, as the blackest."

You need to look no further than Mao Tse Tung, when he said, "Every Communist must grasp the truth, political power grows out of the barrel of a gun." I once wrote, "No man shall ever be debarred the use of arms. The strongest reason for the people to retain the right to keep and bear arms is, as a last resort, to protect themselves against tyranny in government."

Q: How could this happen in the United States?

Jefferson: History reveals how it would happen. You must never assume the words of leaders are honest and have clarity. Beware of the true meaning behind the words. Constitutional scholar Joseph Story wrote, "One of the ordinary modes, by which tyrants accomplish their purposes without resistance, is, by disarming the people, and making it an offense to keep arms."

Another quote I believe is applicable is by Supreme Court Justice Joseph Story, "The right of the citizens to keep and bear arms has justly been considered as the palladium of the liberties of a republic; since it offers a strong moral check against usurpation and arbitrary power of rulers; and will generally, even if these are successful in the first instance, enable the people to resist and triumph over them."

Hitler did not come to power by saying he wanted to slaughter Jews and have an ethnic cleansing. Did he say he was going to war with the rest of the world? Absolutely not. He said he wanted Germany to regain their rightful place in the world, restore German prominence and pride. Hitler and Stalin both gained power by telling people that they wanted to gain "social justice" for all people. The German people certainly did not know his master plans; the country was looking for a leader that would give hope to its people and opportunities for individual success.

Once Hitler gained power and control of its military, it was an easy conquest to take over and rule an unarmed country.

No one would be able to fundamentally change this country by telling the people of his master plan. He would have to deceive the people by eliminating rights by saying that it is in the people's best interest if the government would protect their rights rather than the individual. Saying the rights of individuals would be far better off in the hands of a few rather than in the hands of its citizens is to say that time has changed and these rights are no longer applicable.

Do the schools teach that under communism the Soviet Union starved millions of people in the Ukraine? The Ukraine was the bread basket for the Soviet Union, but when the people did not follow the government's policies, the government took all the grain and sold it to other countries. People died at a rate of twenty-five thousand per day. The government would go door-to-door and collect dead bodies to bury in mass graves. They also took people who were weak from starvation and buried them alive as well. Do you think that if these people were armed for self-protection that the leaders of the Soviet Union would have been able to slaughter millions of them?

North Korea has a stranglehold on its people. The average North Korean is three inches shorter and forty-five pounds lighter than the citizens of South Korea despite the fact they come from the same genetic background. What do you suppose is the reason for the physical differences within the same people? It is obvious that their system is not even able to provide the proper nutrition. Does anyone truly believe that this happened by chance?

Iran controls its people through fear and religion. They are killed or imprisoned if they speak out. Why don't they revolt? Revolution is impossible if you are not armed. They would be slaughtered in the streets.

Would you rise up in revolution unarmed against a country's military might? I think not. In England for centuries the country was governed by kings, nobles, and the ruling class. The people of England had no opportunities to reap the rewards of their labor, to improve their lives or that of their families. They were doomed to remain poor and have their property taken from them. They remained uneducated because educated people think, and through time a leader would rise up and rebel, which had to be brutally squashed by the ruling class. Government feeds on power, and an armed populace helps keep governments at bay.

Toyotomi Hideyoshi of Shogun wrote, "The people of various provinces are strictly forbidden to have in their possession any swords, short swords, bows, spears, firearms, or other types of arms. The possession of unnecessary implements makes difficult the collection of taxes and dues and tends to foment uprisings." Without arms, again, a revolution would have turned into slaughter.

Patrick Henry wrote: "Have we the means of resisting disciplined armies, when our only defense, the militia, is put in the hands of Congress?" John F. Kennedy wrote appropriately, "Those who make a peaceful revolution impossible will make violent revolution inevitable."

Q: What about those who say people are endangered by those who have guns?

Jefferson: There will always be some who will use their guns for evil and some innocents will be harmed. While tragic for the individuals, it is far less painful to society than the anguish that would be inflicted without the ability to protect themselves. The laws must be punitive enough to reduce the chances for violence. If you look at the cities or states with the strongest penalties for crimes committed with guns but also have the most liberal laws on possessing guns, they have the lowest violent crime rates. Then there are cities such as Washington, D.C., and Detroit that have some of the most restrictive laws on owning a gun; they have the highest rate of violent crime.

You must have sufficient laws and punishment to prevent unlawful violence but never at the expense of someone having the right to protect themselves. The right to protect yourself and your family must be paramount to the individual.

Peter Venetoklis said, "Taking my gun away because I might shoot someone is like cutting my tongue out because I might yell 'Fire!' in a crowded theater."

You can look to what Japanese author Yoshimi Ishikawa wrote, "Americans have the will to resist because you have weapons. If you don't have a gun, freedom of speech has no power."

Q: But isn't the proliferation of guns the cause of increase in violent deaths?

Jefferson: There are many reasons for deaths by the use of guns. One of the main reasons for increase in all violence is the alarming rate of illegitimate births in the U.S. Gertrude Himmelfarb in *The De-Moralization of Society* in 1995 reveals some very interesting statistics on culture and violence. In 1960, 5 percent of children were born illegitimately. That has increased to 30 percent in 1991. These figures are across the board of all races and cultures in the country. Obviously the rates are higher and lower for some groups.

Now if you compare the rise in violent crime to the rise of illegitimate births for the same period, you will see that they mirror each other. According to the same study in 1960 there were 1,900 violent crimes per 100,000 people; that increased to 5,700 per 100,000 in 1992. The increase is not due to any proliferation of guns but the moral decay that has grown in the country. In my time almost everyone had guns for a variety of reasons, but the moral and family culture was stronger and that was the reason for less violent crime.

Q: You state culture has changed since your time. Then shouldn't the laws change to fit the times? School shootings are an example many use to say we must eliminate guns.

Jefferson: Absolutely not, just the opposite. First let's not forget the main and original purpose of the Second Amendment is to be able to protect yourself from the government. School shootings are very rare, but the nature of the crime will draw huge national attention to the issue. In today's climate maybe teachers or others should be allowed to carry a gun to protect their students or increase security measures to insure the safety of the students.

Many people every day save their lives or property with the use of a gun, but it brings no national attention. With increased violence you would propose eliminating a person's right to defend themselves? Patrick Henry, I believe, said it best: "Are we at last brought to such a humiliating and debasing degradation that we cannot be trusted with arms for our own defense? Where is the difference between having our arms under our own possession and under our own direction, and having them under the management of Congress? If our defense be the real object of having in those arms, in whose hands can they be trusted with more propriety, or equal safety to us, as in our own hands?"

Q: What about the increase in gun deaths?

Jefferson: People who want to repeal the Second Amendment often cite statistics to support their cause. As has always been the case, statistics can be manipulated to make the case appear sound. According to the Bureau of Justice statistics, 56 percent of all gun deaths are suicides. Do we believe that these people would all choose to live if we eliminated guns?

To expand further, two of three deaths by the use of guns are either suicides or drug related. That leaves only a third of the deaths that are not attributed to either suicide or drugs. What makes up the other third? Crime-related deaths both of the victim and the criminal, accidents, violent or deranged individuals, to name a few.

They do not publish how many people have saved the lives of themselves or their families with the use of a gun. If you eliminated the guns of honest citizens, does anyone believe crime or crime-related deaths would go down? An unarmed populace is like sheep living with wolves and hoping the wolves will change their diet.

I wrote the following and still believe this to this day: "I know no safe depository of the ultimate powers of the society but with the people themselves; and if we think them not enlightened enough to exercise their control with a wholesome discretion, the remedy is not to take it from them, but to inform their discretion." I think Samuel Adams summed it up when he said, "The Constitution shall never be construed to prevent the people of the United States, who are peaceable citizens from keeping their own arms."

7

General Welfare Clause: Government's Role in the Pursuit of Happiness

Q: There are many interpretations of the General Welfare clause in the Constitution. Could you give me some insight into this clause?

Jefferson: Section 8 of the Constitution deals with the general welfare of the United States. This was written to spell out what the government must do to insure that all citizens would have access to things that are necessary for daily living. The general welfare clause was referring to the general welfare of all the people and was never written to promote general welfare of some people or any group of people. We did not want the federal government to have the ability or power to provide resources for any particular group of people or any individual state. They would not have the power to tax and redistribute wealth.

We gave the power to the federal government to coin money and regulate the value of that currency. They have the responsibility to build and maintain roads and post offices. To establish patent and copyright laws so that there would be an incentive for those to find ways to advance science and discoveries as well as encourage authors to write and have their work protected from theft by others. To establish a uniform court system where all would enjoy the same rights and protections as all other citizens.

The government has the power to settle boundary disputes between individual states and has the power to raise and support armies and navies for the protection of the country. The government would also regulate commerce among nations as well as commerce among the individual states.

In no way was the general welfare clause intended that the federal government was responsible for every citizen's general welfare. It was and is intended that all citizens be treated equally and fairly under the law, so that every citizen would have the same opportunity to determine his or her own future, good or bad. There will always be individual successes or failures. Government should not and cannot be the body that determines an outcome; the result comes from self-determination.

Q: That does not seem as if you put much power with the federal government. Can you explain why?

Jefferson: James Madison wrote in the Federalist Papers: "The adversaries of the Constitution seem to have lost sight of the PEOPLE altogether in the reasoning's on this subject; and to have viewed these different establishments not only as mutual rivals and enemies, but as uncontrolled by any common superior in their efforts to usurp the authorities of each other. These gentlemen must be here being reminded of their error. They must be told that the ULTIMATE AUTHORITY, wherever the derivative may be found, RESIDES IN THE PEOPLE ALONE." [author's emphasis added]

I think it is crystal clear that we wanted the power to rest with the individuals of this country and not with a government of bureaucrats or nobles. It is each individual's right to succeed or fail by his own hand and decisions. All shall have the right to an education and to be judged fairly by the courts overseeing the laws of the nation or the individual state. It is not the government's place to ensure the success or failure of each individual.

The strength of a government and a society is the family unit. Government should do all that it can to make the family unit stronger. In most cases this is to butt out of a family's business. When government puts restriction on God, it does not promote the family. Again, government cannot promote a religion, but it can by word and deed promote that we are a just country founded on the principles of an almighty and just God. When government makes God an unimportant factor in its course of action, it promotes man and manmade government and reduces God's impact and the family will suffer.

When government promotes a redistribution of wealth, it diminishes the value of the family and the nation in the long term will suffer.

Q: How does that apply when in the Declaration of Independence you stated that they have the right to life, liberty, and the pursuit of happiness?

Jefferson: I believe that quote of mine is still applicable today, "The democracy will cease to exist when you take away from those who are willing to work and give to those who would not."

The taking from the productive and giving to the unproductive is everywhere in society and has enormous ramifications. The pursuit of happiness has now become, we guarantee you happiness. Welfare is an example of abusing the general welfare clause that we have changed society.

In the past, when there were hard times such as the Great Depression, people rallied around the family, community, and church. Now, as a people, we should help care for those who truly cannot care for themselves because of mental or physical disabilities. However, when people are dependent on the government, they should be required to give back to the taxpayers for their generosity. This might only mean a couple of days a week working for the benefit of the community but it should not be *free*.

I stated once and still believe this: "I think we have more machinery of government than is necessary, too many parasites living on the labor of the industrious." Now there is no need to be self-sufficient because the government steps in and says they will take care of you. This does not encourage a person to strive to improve or even to just survive.

I wrote, "Dependence begets subservience and venality, suffocates the germ of virtue, and prepares fit tools for the designs of ambition." The system encourages the breakup of families because benefits will be reduced or cut off if the family is intact. This is educating generation after generation that there are rewards for not taking responsibility for your own welfare. It increases crime and breaks up more families, which is detrimental to society as well as to the individuals.

All of this was well intentioned, but with disastrous results. When you are dependent upon people you know, whether relatives or community, people out of pride will find ways to become self-sufficient. The family has to be the central unit responsible for the care of each other, not an outside source. Strong individual families create strong communities and a strong moral country.

To paraphrase Dr. Walter Williams, an economics professor from George Mason University, when you give to others personally, you are charitable; when government takes from you and gives to another, it is not charity, it is theft. I agree with Dr. Williams, it is not the purpose or the right of the government to take from one citizen and give to another for any reason. As Benjamin Franklin said, "The Constitution only gives people the right to pursue happiness. You have to catch it yourself."

Q: The government gives tax credits for child care. Isn't that looking out for the general welfare of the people?

Jefferson: Absolutely not! As discussed, there are ramifications to government sponsoring any type of behavior. Does it enhance the family unit by having one of the parents not at home but at a place of employment? Having two parents in the family can also drive down wages thereby making the working two-person family even more important. How does this drive down wages?

If you would take, for an example, 25 percent of the workers out of the workforce, you would have more demand for employees; that drives up wages by supply and demand. Why should the government be in the child care business? I see no reason for it. It is encouraging behaviors and that is not the purpose of government unless it is to help prevent illegal behavior. Does it benefit society that children come home from school to a parentless home? Does it increase the benefit to the student? Does an education standard improve? Does it reduce crime? These are legitimate questions a citizen should ask. There are always ramifications when government interferes with families.

Q: Doesn't welfare give people a chance at prosperity?

Jefferson: It is clear that dependency on another breeds more dependency, not less. The easier it is to have access to welfare, the more people will be on it.

During the 1960s there was the Great Society program. This program was intended to wipe out poverty and raise the standard of living for everyone. What did it do? It increased the number of people on welfare, lowered the standard of living for many Americans, broke up families, and lowered the education achievement levels. Hundreds of billions of dollars poured into the system with disastrous results. Big government never works; it takes away liberty from the individual and puts our nation at risk with massive budget deficits. The answer lies first with the individual, second with the family, and third with the local community. I wish people would not listen to the words spoken by government officials but evaluate the actions and results of the government.

I believe a great example of this occurred when Davy Crockett was elected to the House of Representatives and Congress wanted to give money to a widow of a naval officer to help her financially. This is what Rep. Crockett said to the assembly, "Mr. Speaker, I have as much sympathy as any man in the House, but Congress has no power to appropriate this money as an act of charity. Every member upon this floor knows it. We have the right, as individuals, to give away as much of our own money as we please to charity; but as members of Congress we have no right to appropriate a dollar of the public money. Mr. Speaker, I have said we have the right to give as much of our own as we please. I am the poorest man on this floor. I cannot vote for this bill, but I will give one week's pay to the object, and if every member of congress will do the same, it will amount to more than the bill asks."

The bill did not pass but it is interesting to note that none of the representatives gave one dime of their own money to the cause.

The Founding Fathers were concerned about poverty but almost all agreed that with a level playing field and hard work most people can rise out of poverty. Those physically or mentally unable can be cared for by their churches, charities, families, and communities. Benjamin Franklin wrote that rewarding idleness is a great sin to society and to the person receiving the rewards.

I agree with Dr. Franklin. The following are some quotes from Benjamin Franklin concerning welfare: "Compassion which breeds debilitating dependency and weakness is counterproductive. Compassion, which smothers the instinct to strive and excel is counterproductive." He also wrote about how the poor should be helped. I agree with the following quotes from Benjamin Franklin: "Where emergency help is provided, do not prolong it to the point where it becomes habitual." "Do not completely care for the needy—merely help them to help themselves." Finally, "Give the poor the satisfaction of earned achievement instead of rewarding them without achievement."

As I have stated, welfare also interferes with a family's ability to function as a family. Look back into the 1600s and 1700s in Europe. People lived in squalor, with no education and no opportunities. Now look into our cities and you are seeing the same results. People receiving welfare on the whole are less educated and the numbers are growing not diminishing. It takes away the need to succeed. Existence becomes the norm and stifles the drive to succeed.

I wrote," I think our governments will remain virtuous for many centuries as long as they are chiefly agricultural; and this will be as long as there shall be vacant lands in any part of America. When they get piled upon one another in large cities as in Europe, they will become corrupt as Europe."

Government has a self-serving interest in keeping people on welfare because it keeps them in power. People will vote for those who will keep their benefits coming regardless of what it does to their individual rights and liberties. The novelist Orson Scott Card wrote, "If pigs could vote, the man with the slop bucket would be elected swineherd every time, no matter how much slaughtering he did on the side."

Q: Health care is a current issue facing the country. Is health care a right?

Jefferson: Health care is certainly not a right, and it definitely does not fall under the general welfare clause, as I stated earlier what the general welfare clause does cover.

Rights are given to every man from God. Health care is a good, a product, not a right. A car and a house are both goods, a product. These are not rights. Rights are given at birth; a good is something that must be purchased. A person saying that health care is a right could take that argument to include food, cars, and homes and the list would be endless. Are you allowed to go to the grocery store and help yourself to food? If that were the case, there would be no grocery stores as no sane person would open a store and give away his livelihood to anyone who desired to take his product at no cost.

Why do we have to treat someone who comes to a hospital and says, "I want you to treat me for free"? Health care is a product or a good; it is not a God-given right. Nowhere is it in the Constitution that health care is a right any more so than a car or a house is a right!

There is always a moral obligation of family, churches, and citizens to help their fellow man. This should be done on a local level, never on a federal level. Again, the government cannot take from one man to give to another. The government is there to make sure that all citizens have an equal opportunity to fulfill their goals but not to determine the success or failure of any one. Governments will never be as judicious with your money as you would, as they have no vested interest in the money other than the control it brings.

History of all governments including ours proves that government cannot be fiscally responsible. Look at Social Security, Medicare, or the general federal budget. All run huge deficits due to overpromising, poor oversight, and no fiscal restraints. Government will just tax you more to cover their inefficiencies. Private business cannot do that! If they do not run the business fiscally responsibly, they go broke and out of business. Governments on the other hand just print more money thereby devaluing your money.

Look at the Social Security program. The amount paid into it by citizens was never to exceed 1 percent of their gross income, but look where it is today. The money paid into the Social Security fund was taken and put into the general fund to help pay for all the other government spending, and now they will be paying out more than they take in each year. The whole system is insolvent. If it were private business, they would have been thrown in jail.

A quote of mine is still applicable, "Congress has not unlimited powers to provide for the general welfare, but only those specifically enumerated." I also said, "We are all doubtless bound to contribute a certain portion of our income to the support of charitable and other useful public institutions. But it is a part of our duty also to apply our contributions in the most effectual way we can to secure this object. The question then is whether this will not be done better by each of us appropriating our whole contribution to the institutions within our reach, under our own eye, and over which we can exercise some useful control? Or would it be better that each should divide the sum he can spare among all the institutions of his State or the United States? Reason and the interest of these institutions themselves, certainly decide in favor of the former practice."

Q: What are some of the causes of the rapid rise in health care costs? What are some suggestions for controlling the costs?

Jefferson: Government always has unintended consequences. When wage and price controls were put into place during the Great Depression, business owners who needed employees were kept from offering potential employees more money to attract them. They then got creative and offered benefits to get around the wage and price controls. This allowed prices to skyrocket because the person receiving the medical care did not feel the impact of the rise in medical costs.

When you have a third party paying for medical expenses, or any expense for that matter, prices rise and there is no outcry from the consumer because a third party pays the bulk of the cost. Then you have the expansion of lawsuits filed by attorneys in many cases never intending to go to court because defendants would settle rather than face the cost of litigation. Many times these are very frivolous lawsuits that are little more than blackmail. The threat of lawsuits is estimated to add approximately 20 percent to the cost of medicine as doctors perform many unneeded tests to protect themselves from the threat of a lawsuit. It always comes down to money and power.

Over time people have gotten used to having someone else take care of them and that in itself will be the ruin of the individual and the nation. Everyone must be accountable. People buy new cars, new flat screen TVs, go out to eat, and buy all the things that have immediate and visible gratification. Yet those same people think they cannot afford health care. What is more important than one's health and their life? But people spend so much more on "things" rather than in taking charge of their life and health partly because it has become acceptable behavior.

People make choices, which they are free to do, and some choose not to pay for health care insurance. While it might appear to be callous to say that no one should be responsible for the health care of those individuals, that is reality. People must be free to choose even if that decision causes them to suffer harm in the form of being denied access to health care. Government is not authorized under the Constitution to regulate an individual's behavior, which would clearly be unconstitutional. U.S. Supreme Court Justice Marshall wrote, "History teaches that grave threats to liberty often come in times of urgency, when constitutional rights seem too extravagant to endure."

You must let the free enterprise system work. Let the insurance providers offer insurance across state lines. The insured should have the right to pick and choose the coverages that they wish to have and not have. As an example, if an insured does not want coverage for HIV/AIDS, syphilis, pregnancy, etc., they should not have to be covered and their premiums should be reduced accordingly. The government also has refused to allow insurers to compete across state lines. Why? Surely not out of concern for the citizen.

We need to reform the legal system to control frivolous lawsuits and make the plaintiff responsible for expenses incurred on both sides for these frivolous lawsuits. Have an arbitrator review cases prior to going to court. If the plaintiff or the defendant does not agree to the arbitrator's decision and the suit goes to court, the losers must be held accountable for all expenses.

Put all fees the doctors charge on the Internet so a consumer can compare costs of medical procedures. Put a patient's medical history on the Internet, protected by passwords, so that we can reduce the number of repetitive procedures. This would help eliminate mistakes in diagnosis as well as mistakes made in prescriptions.

Government can make pre-existing conditions and portability available without massive intrusion into the present system. There can be high-risk pools to cover pre-existing conditions, but mandating an insurance company to pay for all pre-existing conditions makes the whole system insolvent. Many would never take the insurance until they needed it at that moment. You can have states set up uninsured programs similar to auto insurance's uninsured coverage.

Beware as governments are neither moral nor just. I wrote: "If the people let the government decide what foods they eat and what medicine they take, their bodies will soon be in as sorry a state as are the souls of those who live under tyranny."

Q: What do you feel would happen morally if the government took control of the nation's health care system?

Jefferson: You will then lose control of your lives. You lose your right to live as you wish to live. You lose your freedom and your liberty. Government will decide who is worth the cost of treatment and who is not. The true cost of medical care lies in the first couple years of life and at the end of life. The only way to control cost of care for the government is to reduce the number of births through mandates from the government limiting your reproductive rights. They also would have people die who are no longer producing for the government and are a liability.

You must look at history, as history will reveal the future. Is there anywhere in the world where government health care has been run fiscally or morally? This country will be no different. Look at Medicare and you see graft and mismanagement and a system that is broken. Now they must increase cost and reduce benefits to try to keep the program solvent. The same will be true for health care.

To give you an example of government's inability to manage even the simplest of programs, look at the cafeteria in Congress. The House has a private company running their cafeteria, and it has been profitable every year. The Senate's cafeteria is run by the government, and every year the cafeteria loses over a million dollars. That is just a simple cafeteria! Imagine what you would have with something as complex as health care.

Fiscally and morally, do not turn your lives, your freedom, your liberty, and your future over to anyone. You must be responsible for your own future and destiny. Benjamin Franklin said, "Those who would give up essential liberty, to purchase a little temporary safety, deserve neither liberty nor safety."

Q: You talk about self-reliance. What about the country's current welfare system? Don't we as a society have responsibility to help people who need assistance?

Jefferson: In many ways it is very similar to the health care issue that we talked about earlier. You are taking the earned bread of one and giving it to another without his permission. Is that legal? Is that morally right? A person would say that it is moral to help a fellow citizen in times of need. That is absolutely correct; however, it is the individual's choice to make that decision, not the government's right to take from him involuntarily to give to another. President Ronald Reagan once said, "Unemployment insurance is a pre-paid vacation for freeloaders."

Q: What would become of people in need if welfare were not available?

Jefferson: The same that became of the people in my time or in the 1800s or the early 1900s! They relied on family, church, and the community for help. When it becomes an entitlement to receive money from the company, you have a complete breakdown of social values. In the 1960s during the Great Society, we saw a huge increase in the welfare state. Some say it was a payment to buy off violence. Would giving money stop increases in violence? To say that people turn to violence because of poverty is not borne out by facts. Violence causes poverty, not the other way around.

When you have violence, you will not have commerce in that turbulent area. No business will trade in violent areas as the risks are too great, which causes high unemployment and high prices for commodities. The businesses that do operate in high-risk areas will charge more for their goods because of the risks involved in doing business in that area. That leads to more poverty as their dollars buy less than in other areas.

If poverty is the cause of violence, why aren't most poor people violent? Are we to think that all companies that are not in the business of making money are just benevolent corporations? I think not. They want profits but with reasonable risks. Violence is not a reasonable risk. In today's age Walmart is the dominant retailer—many say ruthless and greedy. If that is the case, why do they not invest in these high crime areas? Is it that they don't want to take advantage of the poor people? Certainly not, it is that the cost of doing business in those areas is too great, thus the people living in those areas do not have the choice of buying their products or being employed by them.

Q: But what would happen to the family without welfare?

Jefferson: The question should be what has happened to the family because of welfare. Since the 1960s when welfare rolls expanded greatly, we saw a huge increase in illegitimate births. In some communities 70 percent of all births are illegitimate. This is because the system rewarded people to have births out of wedlock and punished them for being a traditional family. This caused a drop in education and an increase in crime. It destroys the basic pride in the individual, which is necessary for a person to strive to succeed. It becomes a self-perpetuating situation.

When you break down the family unit, you break down the community and eventually the country crumbles. The country was founded on self-reliance. This is the most magnanimous country in the world. Communities, families, and churches will help people on a temporary basis and that strengthens the family, rather than destroys it.

President Ronald Reagan said, "Government's first duty is to protect people, not run their lives." The strings attached to government welfare do all the things to break down the family, not to help solidify the foundation. The intentions are well founded but the results are disastrous. We need to be judged by results not intentions. Welfare is a means of enslaving the people to the government, taking from them the liberty that all men have the right to enjoy. When you have people who are dependent on the government, the government becomes all powerful. Those dependent on the government will do everything to keep the power in government to retain their "benefits" even at the expense of their own rights.

History is full of examples of the government gaining control over people's lives by offering to take care of their needs. China, the Soviet Union, North Korea, Germany, to name a few of the countries that have done this at the expense of freedom and the resulting destruction of human life.

Patrick Henry once said, "I have but one lamp by which my feet are guided, and that is the lamp of experience. I know of no way of judging the future but by the past." I think President Reagan summed it up by saying, "Welfare's purpose should be to eliminate, as far as possible, the need for its own existence."

Q: Since we have so much welfare ingrained in our way of life, isn't it impossible to reverse this course now?

Jefferson: In the early 2000s the government had a major overhaul in the welfare system and there were cries of anguish claiming mothers and babies were going to be thrown out into the street and we would have people starving to death. They claimed violence would become rampant. None of this came to pass.

More people went to work, or went back to school, and people found ways to survive and prosper, which is human nature when faced with adversity. Now that the country is going through a horrible economic time, which incidentally was caused by many years of irresponsible government, we are seeing the call to return to more welfare and government dependency. This is exactly the wrong course to take, but it is the easy one. It is also an opportunity government can use this time to increase its power at the expense of everyone's rights.

In hard times people will grasp at anything to relieve the temporary pain, ignoring the long-term consequences. Benjamin Franklin said, "All human situations have their inconveniences. We feel for those of the present but neither see nor feel those of the future; and hence we often make troublesome changes without amendment, and frequently for the worse." He also was the first one to say, "God helps those that help themselves."

That is not to say that as individuals we should not be charitable, but it should be each person's decision and not that of the government. We are the most charitable nation in the history of the world. Keep the government out of it as they are not charitable and they always bring unintended consequences when they attempt to be. There is no way that any government can afford an expanding welfare system, which is an unproductive society. Eventually there would be massive deficits, which devalues the dollar, causes inflation, and destroys a country's economy. Welfare comes at the expense of freedom and liberty.

Remember the words of Samuel Adams, "If men, through fear, fraud, or mistake, should in terms of renounce or give up any natural right, the eternal law of reason and the grand end of society would absolutely vacate such renunciation. The right of freedom being the gift of Almighty God, it is not in the power of man to alienate this gift and voluntarily become a slave."

Q: So you don't believe that the government should tax some for the general welfare of others?

Jefferson: I will sum it up with what I wrote years ago, "To lay taxes to provide for the general welfare of the United States, that is to say, to lay taxes for the purpose of providing for the general welfare. For the laying of taxes is the power, and the general welfare the purpose for which power is to be exercised. They are not to lay taxes ad libitum for any purpose they please; but only to pay the debts or provide for the welfare of the union."

When you tax for the benefit of some, that is redistribution of wealth, which is clearly unconstitutional! James Madison wrote concerning the rights to property as follows: "The personal right to acquire property, which is a natural right, gives to property, when acquired, a right to protection, as a social right."

When you listen to the words of politicians you will see that they do not match the deeds. President Wilson was the first "progressive" President. He spoke of taking care of all men but the actions told the true story. He wanted to eliminate the checks and balances of the three branches of government and have the "elite" rule the country. He firmly believed that the few "intellectuals" could determine the fate of the people better than the individual. He also believed in eugenics—that only the productive people were meaningful. He also re-segregated the military and civil service employees. President Wilson also imprisoned people who voiced their opposition to his policies. But the term *progressive* sounded to most people like a positive thing, to progress from where we are today.

The truth is that progressive came from progressing past the limitations of the Constitution. The Constitution hinders big government, and progressives want to change that. Progressive became so negative that it was changed to *liberal*. Now when President Reagan started to make liberal a negative, they have moved away from the liberal label and back to the progressive label. This is not to confuse democrats with progressives. They are separate entities. Progressives do not believe in the restraints of the Constitution where the democrats do believe in the Constitution just a bit more expansive than what a conservative would believe.

The genius of man is brought out when he is pushed, when there are needs that must be achieved. New ideas and inventions do not come because someone desires that others take his inspiration for their use and benefit. If this was the case, why would we need a patent office? There would be no need as no one would own their own inspiration or perspiration.

I like what Patrick Henry said, "A patriot must always be ready to defend his country against his government." Governments can be like a river. It can erode your liberties so slowly that you hardly notice until it has washed away your home and has divided our country.

8

Freedom of the Press and Freedom of Speech: Why Speech Is the Safeguard of Liberty

Q: I would like to discuss these two topics together as many times they become intertwined. The founders obviously put a great deal of thought into these rights. Why, in your opinion, are they so important?

Jefferson: You cannot have freedom if your voice is to be silenced or restrained. That voice is carried to the masses by the press. As I wrote, "Our liberty depends on the freedom of the press, and that cannot be limited without being lost." I also believe that you cannot have freedom of speech without the right to bear arms. If you have no way of protecting yourself, the likelihood that you would be able or willing to speak out is diminished greatly if not altogether.

In today's world the press would include the printed word in books, newspapers, magazines as well as the radio, television, and the Internet. It is a means of educating and informing others of your thoughts and experiences. People need exposure to diversity of thought. If the government has control of speech or the press, you will no longer have access to information, only state propaganda. When you have revolutions in countries, there is a reason that the first thing the revolutionaries will do is seize the communications of that country. This way, they can control the information given out therefore controlling the rebellion.

I wrote, "Whenever the people are well informed, they can be trusted with their own government; that whenever things get so far wrong as to attract their notice, they may be relied on to set them to rights." That means that well-informed educated people can be relied on to correct mistakes as they see them happening. Conversely uninformed people are at the mercy of the government. When we felt that England was taking the right and liberties from us, we spread the word through newspapers. England's first response was to limit and curtail what we were able to say and print. This caused the educated to rise up and correct the wrongdoings.

Q: When should the government be allowed to use censorship of speech and of the press?

Jefferson: Government involvement has to be extremely limited! Intervening is acceptable only when it is proven that it can be harmful to others. The old adage of yelling "fire" in a crowed place is an example of speech being potentially harmful; pornography that is accessible to children and profane language are a few other examples of where speech or press can be curtailed if it is proven that it can be harmful to others.

The government cannot regulate the quality or volume of speech or press that they deem to be negative to the government. On this subject I have said, "To compel a man to furnish funds for the propagation of ideas he disbelieves and abhors is sinful and tyrannical." The public will decide what acceptable levels are, and they will not listen or read to what they feel has no merit. I also wrote, "All tyranny needs to gain a foothold is for people of good conscience to remain quiet."

Always be fearful when the government comes to you and wants censorship under any guise, whether it be hate speech, fairness, public interest, etc.; they are taking your liberty from you as sure as a thief in the night. I will quote the First Amendment as I think it is abundantly clear the purpose and the intent. "Congress shall make no law respecting, an establishment of religion or prohibiting the free exercise thereof; or abridging the freedom of speech, or the press; or the right of the people peaceably to assemble, and to petition the Government for a redress of grievances."

Following the First Amendment, you can see that there would be very little leeway on censorship that would be lawful by the government. George Washington wrote, "If the freedom of speech is taken away, then dumb and silent we may be led, like sheep to the slaughter."

Q: There are now discussions about a "Fairness Doctrine," where the government would oversee radio or TV broadcasts to ensure that all sides of an argument get equal representation. What would be wrong with that?

Jefferson: I am amazed you would ask such a question. Didn't I just recite the First Amendment to you? Where does it say that someone in the government would have the authority to stifle free speech because they don't like what is being said? There were many publications in my time that offended people. If it enlightens them, terrific, if it causes them to think, terrific, if it enrages them to speak out against it, terrific!

People always have the right to pick up a newspaper or book and read it or not to read it. They also have the right to listen to radio or TV or not. The marketplace will be its own censor. The country cannot afford to have the government dictate what is available to the public and still have an informed and free populace.

Samuel Adams wrote, "A general dissolution of the principles and manners will more surely overthrow the liberties of America than the whole force of the common enemy." Giving the government the power to censor is illegal and would be the beginning of the downfall of this great nation. Who is to censor the government? Do you really think that they do not wish to remain in power? They do not wish to see their power expanded? There is no case in history to be made where a government that controlled speech did so without becoming tyrannical.

I liken it to a quote from Benjamin Franklin, "A countryman between two lawyers is like a fish between two cats." As a citizen, you would have as much of a chance to remain free as the fish does between the two cats if you ever gave the government the power to censor.

I also personally like the quote from Walter Lippman, "What the public does is not to express its opinions but to align itself for or against a proposal. If that theory is accepted, we must abandon the notion that democratic government can be the direct expression of the will of the people. We must abandon the notion that the people govern. Instead, we must adopt the theory that, by their occasional mobillsations as a majority, the people support or oppose the individuals who actually govern. We must say that the popular will does not direct continuously but that it intervenes occasionally."

How can the will of the people be achieved if they are not heard? How can a person know if he is alone or in a majority if he cannot speak out and be heard without fear? How can a person organize his neighbors to rise up against injustice if he is not allowed to speak or write?

Chris Patten once said, "In democracy everyone has the right to be represented, even the jerks."

Q: Can you give me some examples of people losing freedom because of government censorship?

Jefferson: It is the usual cast of characters that we spoke of earlier: Germany, China, the Soviet Union, and currently you have Iran, North Korea, and Venezuela! If you look at Venezuela, Chavez gave credit for his overthrowing of the government to taking control of all media as the key to winning his revolution.

You will have propaganda, not information with a government-controlled media. You will lose the ability to be informed, to assemble, and to be educated. Most of all you will lose liberty when censorship is allowed. There is no country that is free without freedom of speech and the press. Quoting James Madison, "The ultimate authority resides in the people alone!"

Q: What about the Internet? Does that need censorship as information can be made readily available and much of it can be false information?

Jefferson: Do you believe all that you read in newspapers or what your neighbor tells you as fact? If not, why would anyone believe all that they read or see on the Internet? It is each individual's responsibility to decide what he chooses to believe, not that of someone else. The proprietor of the Web site must monitor it to ensure information is right, or he could be faced with lawsuits if his site is defaming someone. He also will not stay in business long if the information is not reputable as he will lose his customer base. The risks of private censorship versus federal are minuscule. There is far greater danger of an over reaching, all powerful government than there is from private concerns.

I would much rather have a media fully against everything that I believe in than allow censorship of the message that they are espousing. I do not fear opposing views; I fear the inability to express those views. Censorship would not stop at any given point. History clearly tells us it will expand into other areas such as email. Would you allow the government to open and read your personal letters? Then why would you allow them to read emails or monitor what Web sites you go to? Never let the government get a foothold into your personal lives as they will destroy it.

Ronald Reagan stated, "Concentrated power has always been the enemy of liberty." He also said, "Man is not free unless government is limited."

Q: Today there seems to be an attack on the blogs—the sites created for people to give their personal views. Some of this is considered hate speech or just attacked because it is misinformation. What are your feelings on this?

Jefferson: I wrote once on this subject, "I am mortified to be told that, in the United States of America, the sale of a book can become a subject of inquiry, and of criminal inquiry too." The blogs today are not much different than what we did years ago.

In the past we would meet in taverns and churches and gave our views. Some of the views could be determined as hate speech by some. We wrote in newspapers and posted messages in town squares for people to read. You cannot silence people's voices. It is the individual's responsibility to determine what is right and what is wrong the same way as when they read editorial pages in the newspaper. Now, obviously, if someone is printing information that can be construed as soliciting people to carry out crimes or are libelous, there are legal recourses against those people without affecting the liberties of all others. Government will use isolated events to strip you of your rights and this again is done to gain power.

Always look at what the effects of what newly made laws will be, who gains power and who will profit financially, and you will normally make the right decision on whether or not you wish to transfer your individual rights to that of another.

Concerning information that is open to the public via Internet, blogs, radio, TV, etc., look back at what I said as it is still applicable today, "Nothing can now be believed which is seen in a newspaper. Truth itself becomes suspicious by being put into that polluted vehicle."

The Internet of today is no different than our posting letters on community billboards. There cannot be any infringement of the right to communicate via the Internet anymore than infringing of a person's right to speak on the telephone or even speaking in his own home.

Q: Why was freedom of the press so high a priority in forming this republic when you state that the information is polluted?

Jefferson: Freedom of the press is vital as the number one watchdog of government and its officials. All should be skeptical of the information being given but without an independent watchdog, we the average citizen would never be able to find out the wrong doings of government and its officials. Government is like roaches in your home, you never see them in the daylight, but when you turn out the lights they scurry about everywhere, unknown to us.

When government has any control of a media outlet such as newspapers or television, as examples, that media outlet must be shut down. Government can never be allowed to invest money for any reason into a media outlet. Any government involvement with any media violates the Constitution. The press in bed with the government is certainly the first giant leap into tyranny. Do not support any type of media that does not question with vigor the government and its officials. Scrutiny cannot be too harsh; it is your family's future freedoms that are at stake. Do not listen to any individual reason for government to rationalize that it has a right to censor or control any part of any media. The government should never use its power to censor or attack the media. If they do, it is because they fear the information that is coming out. Truth will survive, if they are just, they have nothing to fear. It is as clear as a declaration of war upon your Constitutional rights. As I once said, "Questions with boldness!"

Q: Recently the country has gone through a recession and the government has bailed out some businesses. Now there has been some discussion of financially aiding some newspaper companies that are facing bankruptcy. What are your views on this?

Jefferson: This would be the most egregious violation of the Constitution that I can think of offhand. The press has a Constitutional duty to oversee the government, to expose corruption and abuse of power. Does anyone honestly think that this would continue if their existence is dependent on those that they are investigating? Once the newspapers are in debt to the government, they could no longer be a watchdog on the government. They would become the means for propaganda. For the republic to survive we must have a free and unfettered press.

Consider Russia, China, and North Korea, who all have state-run media and look at what freedoms and liberties those people have. If any media outlet is not viable financially, let them go under. The ramifications of a state-run media outlet are horrific.

I wrote, "Where the press is free and every man able to read; all is safe." I also wrote, "Government can do something for the people only in proportion as it can do something to the people." In regard to losing one's rights, we must always be vigilant as it does not come with warnings for all to see.

Listen to James Madison as he was right when he said, "Since the general civilization of mankind, I believe there are more instances of the abridgement of the freedom of the people by gradual and silent encroachment of those in power than by violent and sudden usurpation." Fight with all your might the government involvement with any form of media. Take to the streets so that your fellow citizens hear your voice of warning of approaching loss of liberty.

Q: There has been some discussion lately about the federal government starting its own news agency as a way of getting news out to the public. They have said it might be needed so that they can insure the news is accurate. What are your thoughts on this?

Jefferson: I believe all of the Founding Fathers would say in unison, UNCONSTITUTIONAL!

It would be nothing more than a propaganda arm of the government with no one to oversee it. We would soon have our liberties reduced to that of Russia, China, Venezuela, or any other third-world country. Do not ever be deceived that for some so called emergency or crisis that you would ever give the power of the press to the government. You would be clearly starting down the road to being enslaved with the government being your master.

In Venezuela, Chavez said clearly that the success of his overthrowing the government was that he gained control of the media. He was able to control the resistance to the overthrow because he controlled all information given out to the public. Since the public was not kept informed, it made it almost impossible to form a resistance that would be united and powerful enough to stop him. The information given out was all positive of the revolution and this disarmed the populace. He was able to put out any information he wanted to without it being questioned. The information put out was that he was going to give everyone "social justice." With no one able to dispute his information, the overthrow of the government was easy.

Q: Besides a revolution, what other drastic events could occur that in your view would harm the country?

Jefferson: The government could take control of every citizen's rights if they don't have access to the information needed to oppose the government's will. The issue facing the government right now is whether or not to have a national health care program. This would be instituted with no resistance as no information would be given out that would oppose the government's plan.

Do you think it would be wise to allow the government to institute a program of the size and scope that would affect every citizen without an open an honest debate? This would allow the government to put out only the information that they would want aired and the public would be left in the dark. America could wake up one day and see that they do not have any private options available to them regarding health care; it would be too late as it would already be enacted into law. I don't believe any reasonable person would want to turn that type of power over to any government.

Without freedom of speech and the press, the government could jail any dissenters who would challenge their policies or powers. Again there would be no one to put out the information to the public. It would be total tyranny.

Q: Can you give me any other examples?

Jefferson: When mistakes, abuses, or illegal acts are made by the government, who would be there to report these abuses? Does anyone honestly think that the government would report on itself? Think of something as minor as pay raises for Congress. They used to vote on raises annually, which caused an outcry from many Americans who believed that Congressmen were not deserving of a pay raise. What did Congress do? They made into law that they would receive annual raises without having to vote on it each year. Was that in the best interest of the country? It was done for self-serving interests only!

Now without a free press, they can spend money, do each other favors, take away individual rights, etc., without anyone exposing this to the public and leaving the country with little or no recourse. It is the press that is given the responsibility to watch government and enlighten the public about government abuses. The government controlling the media would lead to massive abuses, even if well intentioned, and take away every man's liberty.

Alexander Hamilton wrote, "A fondness for power is implanted, in most men, and it is natural to abuse it, when acquired." Look at history: has there ever been a government that has not tried to abuse its power? As I have said many times in this interview, abuse can come with good intentions just as much as with evil intentions. You would have all Congressmen serving life terms as they would control information. How would we know if they have abused power, voted against what we believe in or made laws that we feel are unjust or unconstitutional? We could have treaties made that would put this country at risk of war without our knowledge. The ramifications are so massive that this certainly would no longer be the United States of America. As much as we detest the press at times, it is our most important safeguard of liberty.

I once wrote what I think is absolutely the key to this country remaining great and free, "On every question of construction [of the Constitution] let us carry ourselves back to the time when the Constitution was adopted, recollect the spirit manifested in the debates, and instead of trying what meaning may be squeezed out of the text, or intended against it, conform to the probable one in which it was passed." I also wrote, "I have no fear that the result of our experiment will be that men may be trusted to govern themselves without a master."

9
States Rights: How and Why the Founders Wanted States to Be Independent

Q: What is your opinion on states' rights versus the federal government and how this arrangement affects the rights of individuals?

Jefferson: The Tenth Amendment states it clearly. The powers not delegated to the United States by the Constitution, nor prohibited by it to the states, are reserved to the states respectively, or to the people. Section 8 of the Constitution outlines explicitly what powers the government has and that if it is not given to the federal government in section 8, it is then the individual state's right. I will be brief, but will spell out the rights given to the federal government under section 8.

The Congress shall have Power to lay and collect taxes, Duties, Imposts and Excises, to pay the Debts and provide for the common welfare of the United States; but all Duties, Imposts and Excises shall be uniform throughout the United States.

- To borrow Money on the credit of the United States

- To regulate Commerce with foreign Nations and among the several States and with Indian tribes

- To establish a uniform Rule of Naturalization, and uniform Laws on the subject of bankruptcies throughout the United States

- To coin Money, regulate the Value thereof, and of foreign Coin, and fix the Standard of Weights and Measures

- To provide for the Punishment of counterfeiting the Securities and current Coin of the United States

- To establish Post Offices and post roads

- To promote the Progress of Science and useful Arts, by securing for limited Times to Authors and Inventors the exclusive Right to their respective writings and Discoveries

- To constitute Tribunals inferior to the supreme court

- To define and punish Piracies and felonies committed on the high seas, and Offenses against the Law of Nations

- To declare War, grant letters of Marque and Reprisal, and make Rules concerning Captures on Land and Water

- To raise and support Armies, but no Appropriation of Money to that Use shall be for a longer Term than two years

- To provide and maintain a Navy

- To make Rules for the Government and Regulation of the land and naval forces

- To provide for calling forth the Militia to execute the Laws of the Union, suppress Insurrections and repel Invasions

- To provide for organizing, arming, and disciplining the Militia, and for governing such part of them as may be employed in the Service of the United States, reserving to the States respectively, the Appointment of the Officers, and the authority of training the Militia according to the discipline prescribed by Congress

- To exercise exclusive Legislation in all Cases whatsoever, over such District (not exceeding ten Miles square) as may, by Cession of particular States, and the Acceptance of congress, become the Seat of Government of the United States, and to exercise like Authority over all Places purchases by the Consent of the Legislature of the State in which the Same shall be, for the Erection of Forts, Magazines, Arsenals, dock-yards and other needful Buildings

- To make all Laws which shall be necessary and proper for carrying into Execution the foregoing Powers, and all other Powers vested by this Constitution in the Government of the United States, or in any Department or Officer thereof

When the Constitution lays out clearly the rights of the federal government and the Tenth Amendment clearly states that any power not specifically given to the federal government lies with the individual states, I don't see where there should be much question on this issue. We tried to be as clear as possible that the federal government would have very limited and specific powers and that state and local governments would be more able to serve its citizens than a huge oppressive federal government.

Alexander Hamilton wrote: "The State governments possess inherent advantages, which will ever give them an influence and ascendancy over the National Government, and will forever preclude the possibility of federal encroachments. That their liberties, indeed, can be subverted by the federal head, is repugnant to every rule of political calculation."

Q: Are you saying that the states should not be answering to the federal government in most areas?

Jefferson: Yes indeed I am saying exactly that. When we wrote the Constitution, we wanted a federal government that was limited in power. The further away any government is from its constituents, the less they will understand the unique problems of each state. They become less accountable, less responsible, and hungrier for more power.

I wrote, "The true theory of our Constitution is surely the wisest and best, that the States are independent as to everything themselves, and united as to everything respecting foreign affairs. Let the General Government be reduced to foreign concerns only, and let our affairs be disentangled from those of all other nations, except as to commerce, which the merchants manage better, the more they are left free to manage for themselves, and our general Government may be reduced to a very simple organization, and a very inexpensive one; a few plain duties to be performed by a few servants."

How could anyone say the needs for the people of Alabama are the same as for those who live in Maryland or Hawaii? To say that abortion must be allowed across this nation when clearly there are states and communities that would never tolerate abortion. Does the will of the federal government trump that of a community? If it does, we are certainly headed for tyranny. The states and communities must be allowed to choose their own destiny as long as it does not break natural law or federal law. Federal law should deal only with natural law for the individuals and then deal with commerce, foreign affairs, disputes between the states, etc. The federal government should be there to ensure that individual states do not pass laws that are unconstitutional or reduce or eliminate individual freedom.

The following quote from me sums up my feelings, "I am for a government rigorously frugal and simple. Were we directed from Washington when to sow, when to reap, we should soon want bread."

Q: Can you give me an example of a time that you addressed this issue in writing?

Jefferson: "The several states composing the United States of America are not united on the principle of unlimited submission to their general government; but by a compact under the style and title of a Constitution for the United States, and of amendments thereto, they constituted a general government for special purposes and delegated to that government certain definite powers and whensoever the general government assumes undelegated powers, its acts are unauthoritative , void, and of no force. To this compact each state acceded as a state, and is an integral party, its co-states forming, as to itself, the other party. The government created by this compact was not made the exclusive or final judge of the extent of the powers delegated to itself, since that would have made its discretion, and not the Constitution the measure of its powers."

The purpose of addressing the issue of states' rights was to bring clarity to the subject. The states are not subservient to the federal government. Outside of the defined powers given the federal government by the Constitution, the power to govern itself are given to the individual states. Alexander Hamilton stated, "This balance between the National and State governments ought to be dwelt on with peculiar attention, as it is of the utmost importance. It forms a double security to the people. If one encroaches on their rights, they will find a powerful protection in the other. Indeed they will both be prevented from over passing their constitutional limits by a certain rival ship which will ever subsist between them."

A statement I made long ago still reflects my view of the perils of a strong over reaching government, "I own that I am not a friend to a very energetic government. It is always oppressive."

A brief synopsis of how government was intended to operate is as follows:
The individual is the foundation of our democracy. All decisions are left to the individual to determine his fate as long as it does not interfere with another person's right. Success or failure is decided by his or her abilities, work ethic, education, etc.
The family is without question the most important part of a sound government. The family is responsible to educate members of the family and see to their general welfare. The family is responsible to raise their children in what they deem to be moral and ethical.

The township or local community is the next level. They are responsible for local roads, schools, police, and fire protection. They have the power to levy taxes to pay for the services the community wants and needs. They do not have any rights over the family unless there is evidence of legal abuses within the family. Being close to the people they serve, there is a great deal of accountability of local politicians and government employees to ensure they operate fiscally, morally, and ethically to the community standards.

Next is county government which is similar to the city or town government. They are to provide roads, education, judiciary, and services to people who live within the county but are not governed by a local town. They will provide education, roads, police protection, jails, etc., for the people of their county. They have the right to levy taxes to pay for these services.

State government's primary concern is that all citizens of the state are treated equally and fairly under the state law. Set up review courts to ensure equality of treatment to all of the citizens of the state. They also will oversee trade among the states and work with other states to provide roads among the states. They are more limited than the counties and the cities in its influence over the family. They have limited power to tax as most services will be handled locally.

Finally, you have the federal government whose primary obligation is to protect all citizens' rights. This includes court review of potential miscarriage of justice. I have listed all of their responsibilities separately, and it is clear in the Constitution that they are not to add any powers without a Constitutional amendment being passed.

While this is a brief synopsis of each unit's rights and responsibilities, you can clearly see that most responsibility lies with the individual followed by local and county government. Nowhere is there power given to the federal government to dictate to any state with the exception if a state is violating the Constitution. It is important to remember that the federal government was founded by the states; the federal government did not found the states as the federal government appears to believe today.

Q: The government today will withhold funds to the states if they do not meet government guidelines in everything from education, roads, Medicare, etc.; this is called unfunded mandates. Do you believe this is legal?

Jefferson: If the mandates are outside the power given to the federal government in the Constitution, it is inherently illegal. It is abuse of power. Making states dependent on the federal government is against all that the Constitution stands for. I feel that unfunded mandates are the egregious violation of states' rights. They should be eliminated immediately. Where does the federal government get the right to implement policy within a state and then put the burden to pay for that policy upon the people of that state? The answer is that there is no provision anywhere that gives the federal government that right.

If a state desires a program, let the people of that state decide what they want and need and set up a provision to pay for it. While state government is not the most fiscal body either, it is much better and much more accountable to the people. Stop unfunded mandates now if you want to start on a path of fiscal responsibility.

The states are to have much more control of their own direction than that of the federal government. I see nothing positive with a one-size-fits-all for all of the citizens of the individual states. It is impossible for a far removed power to know what is best for every individual and it certainly is fiscally irresponsible. Quoting John Adams, "In my many years I have come to a conclusion that one useless man is a shame, two is a law firm, and three or more is a congress."

Q: What about the federal department of education?

Jefferson; It is not the federal government's responsibility to educate. They have the right to see that every person has an opportunity to be educated in an oversight capacity but not directly to educate.

I wrote on this subject many years ago, "I [proposed] three distinct grades of education, reaching all classes. 1. Elementary schools for all children generally, rich and poor. 2. Colleges for a middle degree of instruction, calculated for the common purposes of life and such as should be desirable for all who were in easy circumstances. And 3rd, an ultimate grade for teaching the sciences generally and in their highest degree ... The expenses of [the elementary] schools should be borne by the inhabitants of the county, everyone in proportion to his general tax-rate. This would throw on wealth the education of the poor."

You can readily see that I viewed education to be a local issue and not federal. The local communities are the best ones to decide how their children are educated and to hold those teachers responsible for the proper education of the students. Education is the key to liberty and the pursuit of happiness, but when you have a central power dictating what is taught, you are well on the way to tyranny.

I wrote, "Educate and inform the mass of the people ... They are the only sure reliance for the preservation of liberty." I also wrote, "Enlighten the people generally, and tyranny and oppressions of body and mind will vanish like evil spirits at the dawn of day."

Q: Can you give me another example of what you believe should be states' rights?

Jefferson: I believe the gay marriage issue should be a state right. The states should have a right to vote on how their communities are formed. What is moral to their community should be determined by them. Constitutionally you cannot discriminate against any individual for their own life choices, but marriage is not an individual right. It is an institution that was developed by man to help society advance through the network of the family.

Since the states license and sanction marriage, they should have the right to determine how they define marriage. They need to decide if it would benefit society or not—if the granting of gay marriage benefits their communities or if they believe that marriage is an institution to promote families and thus their society. People from the outside should not have a voice in mandating inside an individual state.

Another way that the federal government usurps states' rights is with congressional redistricting. The party that is in power redistricts the states in a manner that guarantees that their

Congressmen will be reelected. Some states have passed laws to prevent this but those are few.

An example of how this is done is to take a metropolitan area and make as an example four districts out of that area. The non-metropolitan area could be made up of one district. They make the four districts out of the area that they know historically votes for them thus giving them four seats in Congress, and the other district that historically does not vote for their party seat just one Congressman. By redrawing the boundaries of districts, they are almost guaranteeing their political power.

This is totally against the spirit of the Constitution as it was intended to have diversity and no one party able to dominate another unless it is the free will of the people. This gives Congress a huge amount of power without having to face the wrath of the people. This is a true threat to everyone's liberties. All states should pass laws immediately to prevent this in the future and this would be a step in returning the power rightfully to the states.

Q: What about natural resources, do they belong to the nation or to the state?

Jefferson: The government is there to settle disputes between states, not to pillage the states' resources. The citizens of each state should be making the decision on what is best for them; no third party should be making that decision. One state might be rich in soil suitable for agriculture; another has rivers that can be used for power, another coal, gold, or oil. That belongs to the state and not the federal government.

Again, the powers are clearly defined by the Constitution and there is nothing in the Constitution that allows the federal government to seize property of the states. In the Articles of Confederation, Article IX paragraph 3 it states, "All controversies concerning the private right of soil claimed under different grants of two or more States, whose jurisdictions as they may respect such lands, and the States which passed such grants are adjusted, the said grants or either of them being at the same time claimed to have originated antecedent to such settlement of jurisdiction, shall on the petition of either party to the Congress of the United States, be finally determined as near as may be in the same manner as is before prescribed for deciding disputes respecting territorial jurisdiction between different States."

You will note that it does not refer to the federal government the right of such land. To have power, any government must have the power of the purse. To deny them the power of the purse is to deny them power which the Constitution clearly limits. To give the Federal government the right to and control of natural resources is to give them the power of the purse.

President Reagan wrote aptly, "Government is like a baby. An alimentary canal with a big appetite at one end and no sense of responsibility at the other." I wrote, "I consider the foundation of the Constitution as laid on this ground: That all powers not delegated to the United States, by the Constitution, nor prohibited by it to the States, are reserved to the States or to the people. To take a single step beyond the boundless field of power, no longer susceptible to any definition."

You can also refer to the Tenth Amendment as an example of the Constitution giving power to the states. I also wrote, "That government is best which governs the least, because its people discipline themselves." I would also like to quote James Madison, "The Constitution of the United States was created by the people of the United States composing the respective states, who alone had the right."

Q: So you are saying the states have given rights to the federal government, not the other way around. What are the recourses available when the government usurps states rights?

Jefferson: We anticipated that the federal government would grow and infringe on states' rights so it is spelled out clearly in the Constitution in Article 5. There are two recourses available; first is that there can be amendments to the Constitution, which has been done several times in the past. It requires two-thirds of the states to ratify the amendment and then it becomes law. The problem with this in regard to reining back the powers of the federal government is getting the issue on the ballot as the government will do everything possible to keep it off the ballot.

The second option is much more viable but it hasn't been used. Each state can decide to put an amendment on the ballot individually. This is called a State Constitutional Convention. If two-thirds of the states vote to ratify the amendment, it then becomes law. As an example you could have a far-reaching amendment stating that the states will no longer answer or follow the federal government on any issue that is not Constitutional. This could include taxes, mandates, laws, etc. This would immediately reduce the size and scope of the federal government.

If the federal government today continues to grow and overstep their Constitutional powers this could become a real option. It would be tantamount to a civil rebellion which I believe in this time is needed. I once wrote, "What country before existed a century and a half without a rebellion? And what country can preserve its liberties if their rulers are not warned from time to time that their people preserve the spirit of resistance?"

Alexander Hamilton wrote, "If the federal government should overpass the just bounds of its authority and make a tyrannical use of its powers, the people, whose creature it is, must appeal to the standard they have formed, and take such measures to redress the injury done to the Constitution as the exigency may suggest and prudence justify."

Q: But state laws may not be uniform as it is with the federal government.

Jefferson: Exactly! That is the reason that we wrote it that way, that states would be allowed to be different so that they would meet the needs and desires of their own state citizens. The only requirement of the states is that they would not violate natural or Constitutional law. This is a way to ensure freedom for all.

If one state for example would be taxing their citizens onerously, they could move to another state. If their home state were not providing education for them, they could move. This would make all of the states try to be fair and judicious so that they would not lose their citizens to another state. When we have an over reaching, over powerful and uniform laws and taxation, the people lose their freedoms as they do not have the recourse of moving to avoid the tyranny.

An all powerful federal government is just another form of tyranny. People should never forget that they have the power of the Constitution in Article 5 to give them back their liberty.

10

Taxation: The Need for Taxation and the Need for Limitations

Q: What are your thoughts on taxation?

Jefferson: Taxes are the biggest potential for abuse of citizens' rights. Government can come up with many excuses for creating and levying taxes. There is a legitimate need for taxes to be raised; those again are outlined in the Constitution.

Governments always want to raise taxes for power. The reasons may be disguised as humanitarian, common good, or similar, but mostly it is about power. Without money, government is powerless. All governments want to grow in size and influence. To do this they must create reasons to tax that people will buy into. Like a magician, never trust the words or the exposed hand; look beyond the words and look for the unseen hand, which is where the truth lies. They state that they need taxes to solve problems, but President Reagan summed it up well with this, "Governments tend not to solve problems, only rearrange them."

Look at history. Government has gotten into welfare, but has it solved the problem? It has gotten into Social Security, but has it solved the problem? Medicare—has it solved the problem? Education? Regulation of business and banking—has it made business less corrupt?

I summed up my feelings this way, "We must not let our rulers load us with perpetual debt. We must make our election between economy and liberty or profusion and servitude. If we run into such debt, as that we must be taxes in our meat and drink, in our necessaries and our comforts, in our labors and our amusements, for our calling and our creeds ... we will have no time to think, no means of calling our miss-managers to account but be glad to obtain subsistence by hiring ourselves to rivet their chains on the necks of our fellow-suffers ... And this is the tendency of all human governments. A departure from principle in one instance becomes a precedent for another ... till the bulk of society is reduced to be mere automatons of misery ... And for the fore-horse of this frightful term is public debt. Taxation follows that, and in its train wretchedness and oppression."

Q: Give me one clear example that we can all understand on abuse of taxation.

Jefferson: President Reagan said, "The government's view of the economy could be summed up in a few short phrases: "If it moves, tax it. If it keeps moving, regulate it. And if it stops moving, subsidize it."

Social Security is known by everyone. It started out to be a security blanket for the elderly and surviving spouses. It was not to exceed 1 percent on a maximum of $14,000 of income. Look at it now: the employer pays as well as the employee, which in reality is a double tax on the wage earner since the employer reduces his wages to pay for the Social Security. The program was to put all monies collected into an untouchable fund. Then when the government needed money, they raided the fund, and it is now part of the general tax fund.

How is this moral or legal, but yet government has gotten so large that it has become difficult to hold responsible. There are now trillions of dollars that are owed to the citizens that the government will have to borrow to pay or default in its legal obligation to pay. The money has been spent on everything imaginable with no accountability. All of the Presidents and Congressmen that have been responsible for this should be jailed.

Do I trust government? Absolutely not, as I once said, "Every government degenerates when trusted to the rulers of the people alone. The people themselves, therefore, are its only safe depositories."

I also wrote, "I predict future happiness for Americans if they can prevent the government from wasting the labors of the people under the pretense of taking care of them." As P.J. O'Rourke said once, "Giving money and power to government is like giving whiskey and car keys to teenage boys."

Q: There is always talk about the rich not paying their fair share. Rich do have more. Do you think they should pay more than they do now?

Jefferson: Everyone must pay taxes or they become wards of the state. This breaks down a democracy because those not paying taxes want increases in benefits because there is no cost to them. This keep government in power, but soon the country will collapse on the backs of a few paying everything for the masses.

According to the Tax Foundation, as of October 2007, here is the breakdown of how income taxes are paid by incomes:

- The top 1% of all taxpayers pays 21.20% of all taxes collected.
- The top 5% of all taxpayers pay 35.75% of all taxes collected.
- The top 10% of all taxpayers pay 46.44% of all taxes collected.
- The top 25% of all taxpayers pay 67.52% of all taxes collected.
- The top 50% of all taxpayers pay 87.17% of all taxes collected.
- The bottom 50% of all taxpayers pay just 12.83% of all tax taxes collected.

Now how could anyone argue that the wealthy don't pay their fair share when the top 10 percent pay almost half of all tax revenue paid into the government and the bottom 50 percent pays only 12 percent? The system is not only unfair, it is unsustainable. The top payers will inevitably find ways to hide their income or reduce it to save on taxes. They also can downsize, quit their business, and just enjoy their fortunes. This causes loss of jobs and loss of revenue for the government.

You must allow the producers to produce and enjoy the fruits of their labors. Conversely, the bottom 50 percent will demand more and more services and government handouts as they have no stake in the revenues collected. In essence they want to enjoy the fruit of another man's labor. Nowhere in history has that worked because eventually you have a rebellion or the system collapses from the weight of the welfare state.

Ronald Reagan said, "The problem is not that people are taxed too little, the problem is that government spends too much." Benjamin Franklin wrote, "He that blows the coals in quarrels that he has nothing to do with, has no right to complain if the sparks fly in his face." I think that is applicable to society: he that is not contributing has no right to complain or demand of others.

Q: In your opinion, what do you feel would be the best way for tax collection to insure that everyone has a stake in our country and its spending of our money?

Jefferson: I think there are two fair ways to collect taxes from all of our citizens.
First of all I think a consumption tax or commonly called a sales tax. You could exempt food from this tax; all other products purchased would have a sales tax applied to every purchase. This would eliminate all income tax collection from wages and therefore no more withholding from your paycheck.

Second, I believe a flat tax as the second option, not as an addition to a consumption tax. All people would pay the same rate of taxes. You could have a $10,000 threshold if you desired, in which the first $10,000 is not taxable, thereby giving the lower income people a small break. This would include everyone who earns income being involved in the tax system. The wealthy pay the same percentage but that equates into a much larger dollar amount collected and does not give them the opportunity to write down their income through deductions. There would be no deductions or tax credits to a person's income. Simple and fair!

The other benefit to either plan is that it would eliminate the IRS and all of its abuses. Right now there is almost no one who can read or understand the tax code. The tax code is also used to manipulate our economy and society by giving tax incentives or tax penalties for behaviors. The government now uses the IRS to force people and corporations to act in a manner that they wish by either taxing behavior or subsidizing wanted behavior through tax incentives. The government should not be in the business of encouraging or discouraging legal behavior.

Q: But things need to get done to benefit society and they can't be done without taxes. How do you get these necessary things accomplished?

Jefferson: I hate being redundant, but the only things the federal government needs money for is spelled out in the Constitution. Would any corporation take its profits and send them through tens of hands to an institution that would send it back through tens of hands, each taking a small piece so that they only get 20 cents on the dollar invested back? I think not.

Most things that are deemed necessary by the local and state communities should be taken care of by those local and state communities. Never should we have a one-size-fits-all. President Reagan wrote, "It has been said that politics is the second oldest profession, I have learned that it bears a striking resemblance to the first." There is always more fiscal responsibility the closer the money is to the one who earns it. Governments are not fiscally responsible because it is not their money. George Washington said, "A government is like fire, a handy servant, but a dangerous master."

Take a look at education, which we discussed earlier. The local community should fund and control local education. They can see if the goals are met in terms of student education and where the money is spent. Why would you send a dollar to the government that is earmarked for education, and get twenty-five cents in return when you could keep the dollar locally and benefit eighty-five cents? Along with the twenty-five cents, they will impose unfunded mandates on you.

History is clear, government has never acted fiscally responsibly and there is no sound reason to believe that it will in the future. It is able to continue this charade because it promises to the poor and uneducated. Those least likely to look at history and most likely to listen to false promises are targeted by the powerful. Most issues come down to self-reliance; government takes that away. *Charitable* government giving always becomes a *right*. People have a *right* to unemployment insurance, welfare, health insurance, TVs, homes, etc. It does not end. It is a monster that feeds itself with the help of the government.

I wrote, "In questions of power, then, let no more be said of confidence in man, but to bind him down from mischief by the chains of the Constitution." While government will never say they want people dependent on the government, that is the goal as it keeps the people in power as people will vote to keep them in power for fear of losing their government subsistence. Mark Twain and I agree when he said, "Suppose you were an idiot. And suppose you were a member of Congress; but then I repeat myself."

Q: You state that government wants control and power, and the key to that is dependency. Exactly how does that work?

Jefferson: It is a simple but overlooked system. You create government jobs; no one wants to lose their jobs so they vote the people in power to remain there to insure their job. There are approximately five people who are affected if a person loses his or her job. Spouses, children, and immediate family are some of those people affected by someone losing a job. They tend to vote to retain people that would have an effect on a person's job that is close to them.

With the massive growth in government employment, you can readily see that it is difficult to get people to change the present power structure. Now you have people on welfare. It is the same scenario but exaggerated as people close to them don't want to take on the burden of caring for these people. Now you add retired people on Social Security. They will vote for people who promise them more money even while the system is broke. Senior citizens are the highest voting group by percentage because they fear government can affect their livelihood. That is why when you address the problems with Social Security, it is a kiss of death to a politician, for which they coined the phrase "the third rail of politics." This means, touch Social Security and your political career is over.

Now you take the three groups I just discussed and add them together and you can see that it is very near impossible to effect real change politically once government has its tentacles into the American public. Look at Europe, and we are becoming them. They are trying to get out of their socialist state, and we are ignoring history and moving to where they are fleeing from.

George Bernard Shaw wrote: "A government which robs Peter to pay Paul can always depend on the support of Paul." Benjamin Franklin added, "Anyone who trades liberty for security deserves neither liberty nor security."

Q: Why do you say governments will never be fiscally responsible?

Jefferson: The answer is simple. History tells us that they never will be. We have the government trying to run Amtrak, and it has never been profitable yet they pour millions more into the project every year. We have airports built for one flight a day, why? We have bridges built to nowhere. We build million-dollar tunnels for turtles to cross under the road. We spend tax money to study why overeating makes us fat. We subsidize businesses that the government wants to see succeed, why? If a business cannot make a profit because no one will pay for its product, why should the government subsidize it? We have fraud and theft from Medicare, Medicaid, and Social Security, but the programs go on and on with no resolution. We spend more money than any other nation on earth for education, but our results keep dropping. But we will say the answer is pouring more money into the system.

When it is not your money, you don't care about the waste. Winston Churchill was brilliant when he said, "I contend that for a nation to try to tax itself into prosperity is like a man standing in a bucket and trying to lift himself up by the handle." I will ask you a question to answer your question: Would you give your hard-earned money to a person who has no vested interest in your money other than to spend it on others? Can any reasonable person believe that a body of individuals with almost no accountability will be fiscally responsible with other people's money? Pure nonsense.

Q: You sound as if you don't believe in taxation at all, which would mean that government would not have funds to operate.

Jefferson: That would be an ideal situation but not realistic. That is why we outlined what the specific responsibilities for the government were. To build roads, operate the federal judiciary system, run postal systems, and fund defense of our nation to name a few. But make no mistake about it, they are few!

The primary purpose of government is to protect its people. Taxes are needed to do that. During the Revolutionary War,

General Washington and his armies suffered unbearably due to lack of supplies such as food, clothing, pay, and munitions. At Valley Forge and Trenton his soldiers boiled their boots to make broth to eat. He also suffered some major defeats to the British because he did not have the necessary supplies to wage the war effectively. This was because the Continental Congress did not have the power to levy taxes upon the states to fund the war. This was because the Articles of Confederation did not give them the power to tax the states.

Many soldiers died in combat or died of exposure and disease because of this. The lack of funds could have cost us the war if it wasn't for General Washington's extraordinary leadership. We must never repeat this mistake again.

There should be no more funding for anything beyond that allowed in the Constitution. Most of the spending is for social programs, education, etc., and these should all be handled on the state and local level. If anyone should think that the present system works, look at the national debt, over $14 trillion, which equates to more than $350,000 in debt for every citizen. In my day they would have been tried for treason and hung.

Frederic Bastiat, a French economist in the 1800s, said, "Government is the great fiction, through which everybody endeavors to live at the expense of everybody else." Government has an appetite for power and money that cannot be satisfied. Government through the power of taxation is involved in everyone's lives. Government claims that they create jobs, create wealth, eliminate poverty, and heal the sick. Government does none of these; they consume wealth, cause poverty while stealing the earnings of the workers and promote abortions and now want to decide who gets life-saving care and who doesn't. People turn the power of life's decisions over to a body of people they don't know or even trust so that they feel they don't have to make those difficult decisions.

Government has created dependency, not independency. This will never give people liberty and the ability to pursue happiness. Please read what I wrote long ago as it is still applicable: "I am not among those who fear the people. They, and not the rich, are our dependence for continued freedom. And to preserve their independence, we must not let our rulers loan us with perpetual debt. We must make our election between economy and liberty, or profusion and servitude. If we run into such debts, as that we must be taxed in our meat and in our drink, in our necessities and our comforts, in our labors and our amusements, for our calling and our creeds, as the people of England are, our people, like them, must come to labor sixteen hours in the twenty-four, give the earning of fifteen of these to the government for their debts and daily expenses; and the sixteenth being insufficient to afford us bread, we must live, as they now do, on oatmeal and potatoes; have no time to think, no means of calling the mismanagers to account; but be glad to obtain subsistence by hiring ourselves to rivet their chains on the necks of our fellow suffers. Our landholders, too, like theirs, retaining indeed the title and stewardships of estates called theirs but held really in trust for the treasury, must wander, like theirs, in foreign countries, and be contented with penury, obscurity, exile, and the glory of the nation. This example reads to us the salutary lesson that private fortunes are destroyed by public as well as by private extravagances. And this is the tendency of all human governments. A departure from principle in one instance becomes a precedent for the second; that second for a third; and so on, till the bulk of society is reduced to mere automatons of misery, to have no sensibilities left but for sinning and suffering. Then begins, indeed, the bellum omnium in omnia, which some philosophers observing to be so general in this world, have mistaken for the natural, instead of the abusive state of man, And the fore horse on this frightful team is public debt. Taxation follow that, and in its train wretchedness and oppression."

Q: If you don't agree with the level of taxation on individuals, how do you feel about corporate taxes?

Jefferson: Corporate taxes? Do you really believe that corporations pay taxes? Citizens who use the products pay the taxes, not the corporations. To a corporation it is an expense that must be covered by the cost of their goods. To the government it is another way to squeeze more dollars from its citizens without their knowledge.

I wrote, "A wise and frugal government, which shall restrain men from injuring one another, shall leave them otherwise free to regulate their own pursuits of industry and improvement." It also allows the government to control corporations by threats of regulation and taxes if they don't comply with its wishes. It can tell them what products to make, how to make them and at what profit levels. Is this free enterprise? Is this freedom? Does this system encourage market growth and the introduction of new products and services when the rewards for one's labor and inspiration are confiscated?

Look at Europe, China, Russia, and other countries. Are they innovators in manufacturing, medicine, and the sciences? Absolutely not. They take these innovations and use them after they are developed by others.

You must let the ambitious, the creative, and the inspirational obtain their just rewards. America has always been the most generous and benevolent people in the history of the world. When you take from corporations or individuals, they cannot be as magnanimous as they would like. Government when trying to be magnanimous is inefficient and corrupt, direct charity by the true giver is the best way to help others. If you want to become a third-world country, continue to allow a government to dictate your lives and stifle creative ambitious people through taxation.

Corporations through jobs bring opportunity for the individual to pursue happiness through personal wealth. When you have onerous taxes on corporations, the jobs will not be created, thus hurting all Americans. When you look at why we don't manufacture nearly as many products as we used to and why we have to import more goods, a large part of the reason is corporate taxes. The United States has the second highest corporate taxes in the world, tied with Japan. We average 10 to 15 percent higher corporate taxes than other countries, which means our products cost 10 to 15 percent higher than other nations to manufacture the product. It puts us in a position where we can't compete and that means a loss of jobs here in this country. Fewer jobs because nations with lower tax rates can make products cheaper than we can here in the United States. Fewer jobs mean fewer opportunities for individual wealth and less income for the country because we have fewer working people. History has pointed this out time and time again.

Q: What about states and taxation?

Jefferson: There is little difference except taxation with states is closer to the people so it makes it harder to be as corrupt or as unaccountable as the federal government. The results can be the same for both governments.

Look at the states with large governments, huge entitlement programs, poor immigration control, and high taxes. They are running huge deficits putting their states financially at risk. And what are many of these states doing to solve the problem? Raising taxes! That only compounds the problem. States that have balanced budget amendments and low taxes are doing well. The high taxed states have high unemployment, and it will only grow as businesses will leave those states and move to states with a more favorable business climate. Those states are also losing population as people move for employment opportunities and to an environment where they can afford housing.

One thing many people don't understand is when there is not a climate that is conducive for people or corporations, the successful and wealthy will move. The wealthy are mobile; they can live anywhere, even outside the United States if taxes become so onerous that living here is no longer a viable option. Who remains? The poor remain and without the income from the wealthy the system collapses. The wealthy can only be punished for so long and then they leave and that punishes the poor.

Consider Europe where the wealthy move constantly to avoid the tax burden imposed by their own countries. This is not a healthy environment for anyone.

Winston Churchill said, "The inherent vice of capitalism is the unequal sharing of blessings. The inherent blessing of socialism is the equal sharing of misery." And Mark Twain added, "The only difference between a tax man and a taxidermist is that the taxidermist leaves the skin."

No nation can long survive with an oppressive government with suppressive taxes. Always remember, these oppressive governments always tax and control in the name of *fairness*.

Q: You seem to say that limiting taxes promotes prosperity, education, and freedom, but people still need help and governments are attempting to satisfy those needs. Why are you saying this help must be limited?

Jefferson: I am absolutely saying that we must have a very limited tax structure. High taxes lead to massive spending, and when the appetite is created for government handouts, we will see an uncontrolled national debt. While President, I eliminated the Internal Revenue System and the excise taxes. I also sold public land and was able to pay down by half the national debt that we had incurred from the Revolutionary War.

Let's look at a city here in the United States: Detroit, Michigan. At one point Detroit was considered one of the most beautiful cities in the world. They have for the last fifty years been one of the most pro-government cities in the country. Liberal welfare programs, government housing assistance, workforce dominated by unions, against the right-to-work provisions as examples. The city has some of the highest crime rates in the nation, low graduation rates, low SAT scores, high single family households, lowest property values of any major city in the country.

If social intervention by the government has created this on a city level, do you honestly think it will be any better on a federal level? Businesses flee Detroit creating even more of a disaster for the community as there are fewer jobs and less revenue to spend to build the city. The only people doing well are the politicians, and they keep power with empty promises that the government will turn their lives around. People continue to vote them into office for fear of losing the little that they have. When a government wants power, they keep the people uneducated and hungry. This has been repeated through time for centuries.

Now look at California, and the same applies. Once the shining example of American greatness, it is now in massive debt and will be asking the American public to bail them out of debt with taxes on all Americans. They are mirroring Detroit.

A quote of mine is still applicable, "My reading of history convinces me that most bad government results from too much government." Redistribution of wealth never works and destroys families and society as a whole.

Q: You bring up redistribution of wealth. What is wrong with it?

Jefferson: Besides being illegal and immoral, it is a great idea. It should not be called redistribution, it should be called theft. It is unconstitutional. Patrick Henry wrote, "Don't interfere with anything in the Constitution. That must be maintained, for it is the only safeguard of our liberties."

I have covered extensively already what happens when you give people a guaranteed pittance: society breaks down for those people. I once wrote, "To take from one, because it is thought that his own industry and that of his father's has acquired too much, in order to spare others, who, or whose fathers have not exercised equal industry and skill, is to violate arbitrarily the first principle of association, the guarantee to everyone of a free exercise of his industry, and the fruits acquired by it."

If you are talking about retribution in the form of redistribution, it is beyond my comprehension to see how that could be either legal or moral. With retribution I am assuming that you would be talking about the slave issue. Since I am no longer living, I cannot pay for my sins. If my great grandchildren did not have slaves or sinned against any person, how can you make them pay for what they did not do? There are many people who did not live in this country during the times of slavery, why should they pay and to whom? Should they pay monies to people who were never slaves? Should we pay money to people whom England imprisoned or executed illegally? What about the Irish who suffered discrimination? What about the Italians? The Asians during World War II and before that were forced to work building railroads.

The individuals who suffered these things have legal recourse against individuals, corporations, or even the government. Legally, how does someone who did not suffer personally be rewarded for injustices done to another person? Where does it end? If you research far enough, it might be very difficult to find any race or creed that has not been mistreated at some point in time. Would there be anyone with a history so clean that they should pay to everyone else? I don't believe we would be able to find enough of those *clean* people left that they could possible pay for everyone.

Should a person be penalized now in the form of paying to another man something that he never committed or condoned but must be now discriminated against because of his race? Should a son be sentenced to prison for a murder that his grandfather committed? Do you think this would bring the country together or divide it? Would there be new bitterness against people because of race or creed? I cannot think of much that would be more illegal or immoral and destructive to this nation.

At the signing of the Declaration of Independence Benjamin Franklin said, "We must all hang together, or, assuredly, we shall all hang separately." He was right then and now, if we pit one against another, even in the name of justice, we as a country will all die together.

Iain Benson wrote aptly, "Complete equality isn't compatible with democracy, but it is agreeable to totalitarianism. After all the only way to ensure the equality of the slothful, the inept and the immoral is to suppress everyone else."

The other issue with redistribution of wealth is that it doesn't work. When the Pilgrims came to this country, the country had more abundance of food, water, fertile land and more game than they had ever seen. They decided all would share equally the fruits of everyone's labor. They had everything going for their success except the system. They were dying off at a rate of 75 percent of the population, and soon they would be extinct. They decided to split up the land and each person was responsible for his or her own plot of land and would use their own resources to feed and clothe themselves. In other words they were left with responsibility for their own success or failure. The community thrived. I think that is a great example of why we do not want socialism or redistribution of wealth.

Q: Some are saying that global warming is an issue created to redistribute wealth. What are your thoughts regarding this issue?

Jefferson: Global warming is certainly not a proven science. You can find as many scientists who believe there is no global warming as there are scientists who profess it to be true. There is now evidence that those who are promoting the theory of global warming have falsified scientific data regarding global warming.

Without getting into the issue of whether there is global warming or not, the ramifications of acting on global warming are huge taxation on all modern countries that is so steep that it will affect the economies severely of those countries. It is redistribution of wealth under the guise of protecting the planet. Countries that produce wealth—and it takes energy to produce wealth—will pay to countries that don't produce wealth profits from their achievement.

It is fundamentally unconstitutional. Taking from the rich and giving to the poor has never worked in history, and it certainly won't work now. Every citizen will have to pay a massive tax on all energy they use from gas for their cars to heating and lighting their homes. I would like to know to whom we will pay the energy tax, to despotic dictators to line their coffers? We know from the past with foreign aid that the money does not reach the people.

When you start paying reparations to countries all over the world, money that is earned by one and given to another country, you have lost all freedoms. Douglas Casey wrote aptly, "Foreign aid might be defined as a transfer from poor people in rich countries to rich people in poor countries." Eventually they will try to have a world government as well. When that happens, you will become slaves to a master called government, with no Constitution to fall back on to protect your liberties.

Would any sane person want to be governed by a body of countries of which 80 percent are run by dictators and despots? James Madison wrote, "All men having power ought to be distrusted to a certain degree." Global warming is a means to an end that most people do not comprehend, as it is Marxism disguised as justice for all.

11

National Debt: The Real Threat to America

Q: I would like to discuss your thoughts on the national debt. In the last thirty years it has grown to over $100 trillion if you include unfunded obligations such as Social Security, Medicare, and Medicaid. This is a number that can never be repaid. What are your thought on our national debt?

Jefferson: I once wrote, "I, however, place economy among the first and most important of republican virtues and public debt as the greatest dangers to be feared."

When you spend more money than you take in, the country goes into debt no different than you do in your own home. When you owe money, it devalues your money. Right now the debt is so large that the country will have to make some terrible choices: not fund their obligations that they have promised, raise taxes to the point that people will no longer have the money to purchase their own necessities thereby lowering the standard of living, or have massive inflation where their money is virtually worthless.

None of the three options is good for our citizens. Inflation is a huge scourge on everyone. The price of a loaf of bread could become $1,000 or more. When the value of the dollar becomes worthless, this would allow the government to pay off the debt. But look at the pain it would cost everyone. It could make the country collapse. It could cause civil unrest or even a full-scale rebellion. Crime would soar and there would be little or no public safety. The national debt is a clear violation of public trust.

Q: What in your opinion is the cause of this national debt?

Jefferson: I once wrote, "Never spend your money before you have earned it." Government has a thirst for power. As we have discussed, governments always desire more and more power, the easiest way to gain power is to make a person dependent upon the government.

Social Security was to be a self-funded program. Never was it intended to be a retirement program but a program to help the spouse in case of the provider's death. The age to start to collect these benefits was sixty-two because the average age of life expectancy for males at the time was sixty years. Through time they kept increasing the amount that individuals had to pay into the program and people started to live longer. The government, rather than keeping the money collected in a separate fund for payment later on, took the money and spent it on other programs. They did not keep the money in a separate fund; they put it into the general tax fund.

The government put off the problem of the upcoming short fall so they could maintain power today by financing social welfare programs. This was immoral, and everyone involved should have been prosecuted. They abandoned their fiduciary responsibility for power, which is in effect theft. They would hide this information from the public so they would not have to face up to their own actions. Now we are faced with a peril of our own doing that could ruin this country for generations to come, if not for all time.

Listen to the words of Benjamin Franklin, "But what madness must it be to run in debt for these superfluities! We are offered, by the terms of this venue, six months credit; and that perhaps has induced some of us to attend it, because we cannot spare the ready money, and hope now to be fine without it. But, ah, think what you do when you run in debt; you give to another the power over your liberty. If you cannot pay at the time, you will be ashamed to see your creditor; you will be in fear when you speak to him; you will make poor pitiful sneaking excuses, and by degrees come to lose your veracity, and sink into base down-right lying."

The problem with government is they are never ashamed and have no remorse for lying to the public. What does government do? They, the politicians, will promise more to buy more time so they don't have to pay for their sins against society. They are the wolves at the lamb's door, and we as a society are to blame for allowing this to happen.

Q: How does the government justify to the people the uncontrolled spending?

Jefferson: They create crisis. They manufacture needs. Remember, with government they always claim it is the lack of revenues, it is never their massive spending and unfunded promises of the future. They tell the people that they are unable to care for themselves and through time people will accept that notion. They tell them that if they don't make enough money, they will subsidize them. They tell them that if they don't take steps to protect themselves that they will protect them. If they don't have high definition TV, they will give them money for it. That if they need to take the train to go to work and it costs too much money, they will help them pay for it. If they want child care, they will create a program to help them with child care. The list goes on and on, it's endless.

It does not take long for people to believe all of these things are essential for life and that government is the vehicle to obtain these things. The government creates class envy as a way of selling their programs to the public. They will tell you that since your neighbor has it, you have the right to have it as well.

The government knows that the people receiving these "free" things from the government will never ask, "How is this being paid for?" The cycle does not end, it continues to grow.

Q: How else does the government get away with this outrageous spending?

Jefferson: Through deception and ignorance. They do not want the public to be informed on what they spend money on. They pass huge bills with a large number of riders to the bill. A rider is nothing more than an add-on to the bill that has nothing to do with the original bill. I call them bribes! The riders are used to spend money in a district or state of a congressional member to get them to vote for the bill. This is done time after time and amounts to billions of wasted dollars.

A favorite "trick" of politicians is to attach riders to a bill that is necessary such as funding of the military. The public thinks that they are passing a funding bill when in reality it is passing a whole series of bills under the heading of military funding. The riders would almost never be able to be passed if they were to be voted on independent of another bill. This is commonly called "bringing home the bacon" to a congressional district or state.

Another way they spend money unknown to the public is after both houses pass the bill, they attach further spending called earmarks. Earmarks can be for millions or even billions of dollars and do not have to be reconsidered as prudent as they just are last-minute additions to the original bill. In the private sector they would be jailed for such action.

You might ask, why doesn't the President veto a bill with all of this pork spending attached to the bill? The answer is that he accepts or rejects the entire bill. In the case of funding for the military, the public would be told he vetoed the funding for the military, which would be political suicide and could damage our national security. Therefore, the President signs the bill into law—earmarks and all.

I believe that law should be made to make every bill stand on its own with no riders or earmarks allowed. Some say that would render Congress impotent as nothing would get passed. My answer to that is if the bill cannot garner a majority of support on its own merits, the bill should never be made into law. The people must rise up and demand change to this system and, if that doesn't work, remove those Congressmen who are violating their fiduciary responsibilities.

Q: What must be done to avoid inflation, the raising of taxes, or even rebellion?

Jefferson: First thing anyone must do is to acknowledge the problem. An alcoholic cannot be cured unless he first admits to being an alcoholic. And with cure there is pain and discomfort.

George Washington wrote years ago about the importance of remaining out of debt. "I entertain a strong hope that the state of national finances is now sufficiently matured to enable you to enter upon a systematic and effectual arrangement for the regular redemption and discharge of debt, according to the right which has been reserved to the government. No measure can be more desirable, whether viewed with an eye to its intrinsic importance, or to the general sentiment and wish of the nation."

I will try to find the answers to your question on eliminating debt and avoiding the perils that will follow if we don't eliminate our debts. First of all the government must by law live with a balanced budget. They cannot be allowed to spend more money than what is collected. The only exceptions would be *declared* war and national disasters. *No commitment* of troops without a clear declaration of war by Congress. Then the money borrowed must have a firm repayment plan that is included in the fiscal budget.

Second, we must go through the budget and eliminate *everything* that is not essential. This includes subsidies to airports, agriculture, health care, railroads, arts, and non-essential research. We must reduce the number of government employees. If it is essential, private business will create the means to provide the service. Consolidating government functions will not only reduce the cost but will make them more accountable. We must reduce the number of people on government assistance. It cannot be done at once but it must be done. People must rely more on family, community, and churches. Government should not be in the business of charity, which should be left up to the individual.

Third, we should eliminate the Federal Reserve and go back to the gold standard. This would keep the value of the dollar strong and would curtail spending as they could not just print money on every whim. Section 8 of the Constitution gives the federal government the power "To coin Money, regulate the value thereof ..." What they did by taking the country off of the gold standard and creating the Federal Reserve was to usurp the Constitution. The Federal Reserve is not a government agency, yet it is allowed to make money available through banks without directly printing the money. This in my opinion is unconstitutional.

Fourth, we should eliminate all unfunded mandates from the government to the states. The federal government should not be allowed to get around their budget issues by either printing money or by passing responsibilities on to the states. If the states wish to have a particular program, that individual state can pass the law and fund the program themselves. If all fiscal and constitutional programs were followed, you could see a massive reduction in federal taxes and a smaller increase in state taxes. The fewer hands that touch the money, the fewer dollars that will be wasted!

The states should have more power and control than the federal government. The closer you get to the people, the more control the people will have over the government. Remember that the Constitution is a restrictive document; it gives limited power to the government, it restricts the power of government for a purpose—to maintain the liberty of the people. It is not a living breathing document as some have said; the only way to change the Constitution is through Article V, which requires a two-thirds majority to amend the Constitution. The Constitution was never intended to state what the government can do with the exception of those items listed in Section 8, which I stated earlier.

Fifth, I would return the rights to the states to oversee and control their natural resources. This includes water, land, air, oil, coal, natural gas, minerals, etc. This would create a competitive environment that would create jobs and increase revenues. If a state would offer more opportunity and freedom to business or individuals, they would move to that state. States would be forced not to over-burden their constituents with regulation or taxes for the fear of losing their population. By allowing the states to use their natural resources, as they have the right to do so, would reduce the cost of energy thereby making our products cheaper and more competitive. The jobs created would improve quality of life, increase tax revenues without increasing their rates, and the money raised could be used to pay off our debt.

We must consider ourselves drug addicts. Everyone must own up to our problem as a nation. We will go through withdrawal. We will have times of pain and anguish, but there is a light at the end of the tunnel. I wrote, "It is incumbent on every generation to pay its own debts as it goes. A principle which if acted on would save one-half the wars of the world."

Do we wish to go through the pain of withdrawal, or do we wish to curl up in a corner in the fetal position waiting to die?

Liberty is a wonderful thing; it produces wealth and harmony and strengthens the pursuit of happiness. As citizens we must remember it is each of our responsibilities to be informed of our government activities and hold all those that do not follow the Constitution accountable. The Constitution gives the people the power. They have the power and obligation to use that power when deemed necessary to protect our nation from abuse of power from our own government. When right, never fear from acting!

12

Immigration: Can Immigration Destroy America Without Firing a Shot?

Q: Immigration is a huge issue today. Some want everyone to be able to come into our country and others want very strict control. What are your thoughts regarding this issue?

Jefferson: First of all you cannot have a sovereign nation without controlling its borders. Who are the citizens of a country if there is not control on who enters? How can you plan for the general welfare of its citizens without the knowledge of the numbers and the needs of the people within its borders?

You have schools, road, health, housing, crime, language, and fundamental beliefs issues that can become insurmountable. A nation must be bound together first by a common language and then by a common belief system in what justice and freedom are. When you have people coming and going, how do you retain these? You will form different cultures and languages within your own nation; this will lead to unrest and eventually violence within our own country.

Immigration must be controlled, and people coming to this country must meet basic standards regarding language and belief systems. You cannot allow people who are uneducated and unskilled who do not speak the English language to come to the United States at will. They will become a burden on society that no nation can afford. You will have resentment from those citizens who will be required to pay for those who come here but cannot fend for themselves. This will divide a nation, not unite it.

Q: You say they must speak the language and have skills that are applicable to our society. What about those fleeing tyranny?

Jefferson: Within reason, this country will give asylum to those who are truly fleeing their own homeland under the threat of death or enslavement. We cannot however open our borders to the world for all those that wish to come here for financial reasons or to share in our wealth. We are a magnanimous country but we cannot afford to care for every person in the world who desires to come to the United States. Those who come here for asylum must come to improve all of our lives and work to improve his or her skills so that they can become a productive part of our society. Those who do not must be returned to their country or to another country that would accept them. This might sound harsh, but it is clear that if you do not have standards to be met, none will be reached.

Q: What about what we call the guest worker program?

Jefferson: It must be limited in scope, and those who do come under this program must know that they must return to their home country on a scheduled basis. They also must know that they do not have Constitutional rights as they are not citizens of this country. Yes we will provide them protection from violence or human abuses, but they do not have the rights to our education system, to vote, to our justice system, to government benefits, etc.

If an American wants a job that a guest worker has and is willing to do the same work for the same money, the job must be given to the citizen. If a guest worker is found not to be law biding, he or she should be deported immediately. As a citizen of this country our allegiances should be to this country. A person coming here for economic opportunity typically does not have allegiance to our country but to his or her own. This is not healthy for our country.

If immigration goes unchecked, we will surrender this country to others and take the liberties and customs of the country from its own citizens. When immigration is controlled, people will be absorbed into our culture, but uncontrolled we will surrender our culture, our laws, and our way of lives to others without ever having a war. The first duty of a government is to protect its citizens, and uncontrolled immigration is certainly a failure of government in its moral and legal obligation.

Q: What is wrong with bringing in new languages in this nation?

Jefferson: Being bilingual is good for any person. I could read and speak many languages, but every citizen needs to have a common language. Can you imagine a family speaking different languages? How would they communicate, how would they educate each other? Do you think it would be good for the family or do you think the family would dissolve? I think the answer is obvious. It is no different for a nation. A family has to be able to communicate. How is a person going to be able to gain employment, go to school, and be treated fairly?

We cannot have fifty different languages and have equality and have a nation united as one with people speaking different languages. A nation must have one language. If a person or group of people comes to this country and insists on speaking their native language, are they saying that they want to bring their former country to this land or are they now becoming patriots of the United States? I think the answer is clear: they are not patriots, they are looking to enrich their lives off of the American system without ever becoming true patriots of this country. We must teach English in schools, and other languages can be taught on an elective basis.

All contracts and commerce must be done under one written and spoken language. If not one language, you have pockets of communities appear that are essentially not a part of the United States. They develop their own economies, their own schools and own customs. This is not to say that people cannot celebrate their heritage, their own customs, but it is to say that all people who come here must come here with the idea of becoming an American and of being absorbed into our culture. We must preserve American society.

Q: Would that not be discriminating against the unskilled immigrant?

Jefferson: Yes if you want to use discrimination as a term of requirement. In the late 1800s and the early 1900s, most immigrants came with skills that improved our society. They came from all parts of the world and brought skills. They were machinists, scientists, writers, educators, steel workers, etc. These people added to our society. When you allow unskilled to pour into our country, they become dependent upon the successful; they pull from society rather than adding to it. In today's age of welfare and unemployment benefits, they consume vast amounts of resources that others will have to pay for. This causes culture breakdown and cultural divide. People do not have a natural right to come to this or any other country.

If we need fences to protect this country, so be it. We do not force anyone to live within our borders, they are free to leave at any time for any reason. Other countries build walls to keep their people from leaving, but that is not the case with this country. Any wall or fence would be only for the purpose of stopping people who we do not know or might not want from entering this country.

Q: The Fourteenth Amendment says that all persons born or naturalized in the United States are citizens of the United States. Do you disagree with this amendment?

Jefferson: I think it was poorly written and do not believe that it was intended to give citizenship to a baby born to people in the United States who are non-citizens. This has caused massive problems with illegal aliens in this country. A person sneaks into this country and has a child who is now a citizen? The baby has all the Constitutional rights, but the parents do not and are subject to deportation? We are now in the business of breaking up a family? No, we now allow the parents to remain illegally. What a colossal mess.

In 1970 one in twenty-one people in the country was an immigrant, in 2007 it is one in eight. That is according to the U.S. Census Bureau statistics. If that trend continues, you can readily see that natural citizens will be the minority. Do you think it will be possible that the country will remain as it was founded? That our language will remain English? That we will keep our customs or even our liberty and rights? They will bring their own constitution to this country without ever firing a shot.

I believe that we must clarify the Fourteenth Amendment and let the people of this country ratify it so there can be no misunderstanding by government or by our court system.

Q: Are you overstating it when you say immigrants will control our country?

Jefferson: Not at all. It takes 2.1 births per woman just to maintain our present population. When the birth rate drops below that, you will have a reduction in population. In the United States now we have approximately 2.2 births per woman. But if you take our immigrants, it is 1.6 births; immigrants have a birth rate of approximately 2.7 per woman.

You can readily see that in a short period of time, natural citizens will be the minority. When natural citizens are no longer the majority, the country as we know it will no longer exist. You must remember that if you don't have control of your borders, the country will be overrun with people trying to enter the country. Look at history, people are not fleeing countries that offer freedom and opportunity; they flee socialist states, dictatorships, and tyrants.

The Soviets did not build the Berlin Wall to keep people out of East Germany; they built it to keep the East Germans from fleeing to West Germany and freedom. Mexico does not have to build walls to keep Americans from crossing the border en mass to live in Mexico! People will always want to flee from those places to countries that offer freedom and opportunity, but no country can survive with open borders for all to come here as they please without the country collapsing in the end from the burden that they create.

Government's first obligation is to protect its people through the Constitution and with its present laws they are abdicating that responsibility.

President John F Kennedy wrote, "Today we need a nation of Minutemen, citizens who are not only prepared to take arms, but citizens who regard the preservation of freedom as the basic purpose of their daily life and who are willing to consciously work and sacrifice for that freedom."

Q: There are many industries such as agriculture service industries that say they need illegals or the guest worker program in order to offer low priced, high-quality products. What are your thoughts on this?

Jefferson: That is ridiculous. First of all you drive down the entry-level wages for our own citizens as they typically pay minimum or below minimum wages to these people. With an artificial expansion of the labor pool, wages are lower than they should be, and you are not letting the free market work.

Without this pool of workers, yes, they would have to pay more for employees, and with fewer workers all citizens benefit from a competitive job market. The allowing of employers to bring in people who are not legal residents should be stopped by enforcing the laws that we have now. Fines that are levied against employers for hiring illegal immigrants would stop this quickly and efficiently. All people would benefit.

Q: How does illegal immigration cost taxpayers?

Jefferson: Where does it not cost Americans? For schools it becomes a nightmare as it holds everyone back as teachers have to spend more time trying to teach them the language and then getting them up to the same level as our students. This costs a huge amount of money as well as our future because our students don't get the proper education they need and deserve.

They use our medical services and seldom are covered by insurance or have the income to pay for the services. Who pays? The American taxpayer! In law enforcement, crime goes up, the public is less safe, we have to have more law enforcement officers, more jails, more court time, legal defense and then more prisons. Most of these are poor people with limited education who come here illegally. This means they will be more likely to need assistance from the government such as housing, welfare, etc.

Look at the terrible financial mess that California is in, and most of it is due to uncontrolled immigration. They have allowed people to enter the state unchecked. These people represent a huge drain on the economy as they have a higher percentage of the people on welfare and in the prisons. They do not come with the background or financial means to be independent citizens. The percentage of these people becoming citizens continues to fall, which indicates two things: first, they do not look at the United States as their country, and second, they are not equipped to compete in this environment.

We are not a nation of immigrants as has been said over and over. That was true two hundred years ago, but since then immigration has been controlled so that they can assimilate into our populace. The government operates with the approval of its citizens, so if you allow rampant uncontrolled immigration, the government will be controlled by immigrants who do not understand or appreciate our culture.

George Washington talked of assimilation, that we must ensure that those who come have American patriotism not patriotism to their mother country.

Q: If immigration that is not controlled can have harmful effects on the country, why would government officials push for increased immigration?

Jefferson: I probably sound like a broken record, but it always comes back to the same thing: power! If you can be viewed as the party that promotes legal and illegal immigration and are promoting full rights and benefits to those immigrants, who do you think those people are likely to vote for? The politicians are looking to guarantee their place in government, and the easiest way to do that is to increase the number of people who are dependent upon the government. So if you can ease or eliminate immigration restrictions, you will increase your voter base thereby increasing your power.

Politicians will achieve their goals by playing the race card. If you oppose illegal immigration, they will try to label you as a racist. They will say that you are not compassionate and you want to keep people who need a place to come and work to feed their families from coming to the country. The thing that most politicians fear is being labeled a racist, so they don't speak out as loudly as they should on opposing illegal immigration.

I have said this over and over during this interview: government thrives on power and will do almost anything to achieve and keep it. They are not being humanitarians; they are selfish narcissistic individuals who put their own power and position above the needs of their own country. Patriots, they are not!

13

Free Market vs. Government Control: Why Government Creates Problems, Not Solves Them

Q: Can you give me a brief explanation of the free market system?

Jefferson: The free market system is the ability of individuals to produce goods that people want or need. The price they will pay for those goods or services will depend on the cost of producing those goods and services and the availability along with competition.

Free markets rise traditionally in this fashion. An entrepreneur will have an idea and be willing to take a chance and invest his money into this idea. If the business is successful, he normally will need to hire managers and salespeople to help him run his business. He will also hire laborers to produce the products. Now the business owner, having taken the risks, will earn the most money from the corporation. The managers and salespeople will earn less but will typically earn a good living. Now the laborers will be paid less, and the amount they are paid will be determined by their skill level. An example is an electrician who will earn more than a janitor.

Typically with laborers is that some will be interested in moving to management, which can happen with hard work and increased responsibility. Winston Churchill summed up the free market system very well, "The inherent vice of capitalism is the unequal sharing of the blessings. The inherent blessing of socialism is the equal sharing of misery."

Q: That makes sense with the production of saleable items but what determines the cost of buying these items?

Jefferson: The amount of money that it takes to produce each item, including packaging, shipping, and marketing the product. The amount of competition for that item and of course the availability. For example, if you are producing shoes, there is a lot of competition and availability. The manufacturer would produce millions of shoes with a small profit margin on each pair, but with millions being sold, his profit would be high. The more competition he has, he must sell his shoes for less profit in order to remain competitive.

If however you were selling nuclear reactors, the demand would be minimal so the profit would have to be extremely high on each reactor in order to produce the profit necessary to continue in business.

As products become more common place, the competition rises and prices fall. An example of this would be the calculator. When first produced the cost per calculator was over one hundred dollars, and it would only add, subtract, multiply, and divide. As the product developed and competition came about, the price dropped to where that same calculator is given away as a promotion item rather than being sold. The new calculators do almost any type of mathematical process, and the cost is less than the original item that could only do basic functions.

The key is letting the entrepreneur have freedom to make a profit. By doing so, he will employ people, thereby creating income for those individuals as well as creating customers for his products. Profit is necessary and should be unrestricted. The marketplace will determine his return on his investment.

All of this increases the standard of living. More employment, cheaper products, and even more tax revenues as more people work thereby contributing to the tax base versus drawing from the government coffers.

Q: But what if business becomes so large that they eliminate competition?

Jefferson: History shows us that competition always rise up when the market feels that they are being charged too much for a product. Take a company such as Microsoft. They were accused of having a monopoly on personal computer operating systems and thus the software that comes with it. Breaking up Microsoft would not have done anything to benefit the consumer. Now we have the reemergence of Macintosh and the growth of Google, which is now making software as well. Prices have gone down greatly on PCs and software as well.

As long as a business is operating legally and is not doing anything illegal to make products unavailable, they should be able to continue to operate and grow. As I stated earlier, most corporations that get so large they can't respond to the marketplace began to fail and will ultimately have to downsize or cease to operate. There are always companies formed to fill a void when a corporation does not meet the demands of the public for quality and price. Profit is the driving force behind capitalism and that profit should not be contained or controlled by government.

Thomas Swell wrote, "Socialism in general has a record of failure so blatant that only an intellectual could ignore or evade it."

Q: You seem to be a believer in the free market system, but doesn't business have to be controlled or there would be massive abuses?

Jefferson: Businesses cannot operate illegally; they cannot be allowed to break the law. Businesses must produce a service or product people desire, and then for them to be successful it must be affordable. The important part of regulation of business is that it be moral to the community it serves. This is local and not federal. If a community deems something moral, it should be allowed to operate within the boundaries of that community.

An example of this would be Nevada, which has allowed gambling and certain counties allow prostitution. Most communities throughout the land would not allow either of these types of endeavors. However, in most cases the free market system will work.

I wrote, "Agriculture, manufactures, commerce and navigation, the four pillars of prosperity, are then most thriving when left most free to individual enterprise." Let us say that a man opens a business and sells hardware. He sells the poorest products at the highest prices. People are unhappy with the products and feel they have been cheated. How long do you believe he will stay in business? Not long, why? The answer is simple: someone will start a business selling a better product at a lower price. No business can long survive if they are not honest and deliver a product or service at a price that is fair and desired by the public.

I once said, "Money and not morality is the principle of commerce and commercial nations." What I meant by that was business is in business to make money, which provides the capital to create more employment, which benefits all men. I also said, "An honest man can feel no pleasure in the exercise of power over his fellow citizens." If he ceases to be moral in his business dealing, the marketplace will correct or eliminate his business. Making money is not immoral, for without it there is no commerce and therefore society fails and we have tyranny.

Let's look at a great example of the free market system versus state-run countries. The Soviet Union in the 1970s and 1980s was importing over 50 percent of their food. This was happening despite having a vast country with rich fertile land. What was the problem with agriculture in this country? Agriculture was controlled by the government. Farmers were told what to grow and how much they would be paid. This led to massive under-production as there was no incentive for the farmer to produce more high-quality products. In the Soviet Union about 3 percent of the land was allowed to be farmed under the owners' control and profits were given to the farmers who owned the land. That mere 3 percent of the agriculture land produced 25 percent of the nation's farm products.

Now in the United States we produce enough to feed the entire world. I think this points out clearly what happens when you take away incentive to produce or create from individuals. You have a population that does the opposite—no production and everyone pays the price for this intrusion into the human right to own property and prosper from their efforts.

Q: What is your opinion on price controls?

Jefferson: This has been tried many times with disastrous results. When you put price controls on commodities it invariably leads to scarcity of those products. The reason is that profit is controlled, and therefore you have fewer people interested in making the product so the product becomes less available.

You also will see an increase in crime as people will supply the product illegally for a higher price to those people who either want or need them. Man will find a way around government control. Government should not set prices nor should they subsidize industry that is struggling to make a profit, but government says that it is essential to people. An example of this is with the farming and dairy industries. Government pays farmers and dairymen at times not to produce so that the prices will stay high. Does this benefit the nation? No, it pays for nonproductive industry and stifles competition and the consumer and taxpayer loses.

Q: In banking, since they handle the nation's capital, shouldn't government regulate the banks' dealings to make sure they operate justly?

Jefferson: Justly? As determined by whom. Again, if a bank does not operate in a way that will benefit their community, the competition will grow and drive him out of business.

Money is another product, another service. People will not give their money to an institution that steals from them. They will not deposit their money in that bank, and the bank will have no money to lend and therefore goes out of business. If they steal, there are laws and they can be punished. If they are just poor businessmen, they will fail. Banks should be kept small and should be kept to a state level so that they cannot become so large that they have the power to dictate to its investors. If banks are allowed to grow to where they have too large a percentage of a nation's resources, we would become slaves to the banks. We do not need a government to dictate their practices as long as they do not violate the Constitution by discriminating against one person in favor of another. The place for the government is not to let any bank or business become so large that they have a monopoly.

John Adams wrote the following concerning his views on banks, "Banks have done more injury to the religion, morality, tranquility, prosperity, and even wealth of the nation than they can have done, or ever will do good."

Q: But what about the government's ability to print money to make it available through the banks?

Jefferson: I wrote: "The system of banking is a blot left in our Constitution which, if not covered, will end in their destruction ... I sincerely believe that banking institutions are more dangerous than standing armies; and that the principle of spending money to be paid by prosperity ... is but swindling futurity on a large scale."

I am referring to the government monetary system of printing money in hopes that the future will bring prosperity to pay the debt incurred. Government's ability to print money without a standard to base the value of that money is irresponsible and would eventually lead to the collapse of a country's financial system. The government borrowing money by printing money is irresponsible, and all citizens should reject any pretense of this with the exception of war to provide for the country's salvation.

In the case of debt incurred for war in the protection of this country, the debt repayment must be the highest priority. Printing money for general welfare of its citizens must not occur. I want to make it clear that is the meaning of when I said fear banking more than a standing army.

My belief is stronger today than yesterday when I wrote these words, "If the American people ever allow private banks to control the issue of currency, first by inflation, then by deflation, the banks and corporations that will grow up around them will deprive the people of all property until their children wake up homeless on the continent their fathers conquered." The Federal Reserve Bank is a private bank that does exactly that and has caused the housing and economic problems this country faces today.

Q: But with government being involved, doesn't that make credit more readily available to all citizens on a more equitable basis?

Jefferson: The government got into the lending business with Fannie Mae and Freddie Mac. As the two largest home loan lenders in the country, they are private firms backed by the federal government. That makes no sense and has caused the biggest economic calamity that this country has faced. They instructed the lenders to offer poor-credit-risk people homes with no down payments, poor credit, and questionable income homes at the lowest rates available. All this was done with the best of intentions—getting everyone who wanted a home, a home.

The American people were guaranteeing these loans without ever knowing it. This had a huge effect on the value of homes and on what people believed was equity in their homes—equity that they could retire on. The opposite happened. The value of homes crashed, and people are losing their equity and net worth.

On the other side, the people they were trying to get into homes are being foreclosed on and losing their homes that they should never have been able to buy. This has caused banks to fail and government to step in to buy them out with money they have borrowed from future citizens, thereby diminishing every citizen's worth and increasing their debt to the government. Who was helped? Who was hurt? Everyone is the answer to a well-intentioned government intervention into the private market system.

President Reagan saw this coming when he said, "Refinance now and save—No SSN required, get 4 free quotes—saves now!" He also said, "Government does not solve problems; it subsidizes them."

Q: Could you tell me in a little bit more detail how this happened with the housing industry?

Jefferson: Under President Jimmy Carter, the government passed the Community Reinvestment Act. This required banks to lend money in areas that were designated to be poor areas, typically inner city areas. If the bank refused to lend money in these areas, the government could pull their charters and close the banks. The banks tried to lend money but in many cases were unable to because the clients in those areas did not meet the banks' lending criteria.

For years, the lending standards of the banks limited the exposure to losses for the banks. Then the government decided to get Fannie Mae and Freddie Mac involved. They instructed Fannie Mae and Freddie Mac to lower their lending standards so that when local banks made these questionable home loans, the local bank could sell them to Fannie Mae or Freddie Mac who would guarantee the loans. Guess who was really guaranteeing these loans? The taxpayer, and without his consent or knowledge. This created a massive, trillion-dollar portfolio that was not built upon sound credit policies; it was based on the taxpayers' back.

When the bubble began to show signs of cracking in the early 2000 years, the government refused to audit the companies because they were afraid the program and its problems would be exposed. They declared publicly that Fannie Mae and Freddie Mae were sound and continued to push Fannie Mae and Freddie Mac to make more of these home loans.

I wrote once, "A wise and frugal government, which shall restrain men from injuring one another, which shall leave them otherwise free to regulate their own pursuits of industry and improvement, and shall not take from the mouth of labor the bread it has earned. This is the sum of good government, and this is necessary to close the circle of our felicity."

A government restrained from regulating for a goal that they wish on society is the key to what I wrote. I ask you, would the country be in its present state financially if the government practiced restraint? Government tends to want to be judged by their intentions rather than its results.

Q: Could you explain how making loans to low income, poorly qualified people had such a massive effect on our economy?

Jefferson: There is a snowball effect. The person who owns say a $100,000 home and intended on staying in the home and paying for it was now being offered $120,000 for his home due to supply and demand. The demand was created by the government because it took a supply of non-qualified applicants and gave them access to the entry-level home. Those people needed properties to buy, so with the increase demand, prices went up.

Now the person thinks he made 20 percent on his home so he buys a home for $150,000 that was also inflated by the artificial demand. This continues all the way up to the homes that are worth millions. When artificial demand is created, the most logical thing that happens is that eventually no one can afford a home because the values are too high for anyone to purchase. When that happens the market falls and the values of the properties fall and people lose what they believe was an asset.

In this particular case, what caused the market to fall was not only the over-inflated values but people who were unqualified began to lose their homes. This caused an oversupply of homes, thus causing the values to fall through the floor. This all happened because government decided to intervene in the free market system because with "good" intentions, they wanted people who were unqualified to be able to buy a home.

Q: How else did it affect the economy?

Jefferson: Well, over the years the government allowed big banks to keep acquiring smaller banks. These banks became enormous. They also created Fannie Mae and Freddie Mac. When people began to default on their homes because they were unqualified, it exposed the banks to massive losses. Now with the huge increase in foreclosures making other homes less in value, people owed more on their homes than they were worth. Many people decided that rather than take the loss of equity, they would give the bank their home back and would start over. This again, contributed to a massive amount of vacant homes further driving down the values, which created even more losses for the banks.

These banks became "too large to fail." The government, fearing that the banks would fail, and thus not have money to lend for homes, cars, and credit cards, decided to "bail out" the banks with taxpayer money. Another problem was created because of irresponsible spending in the past; the government did not have enough money to bail out the banks, so they had to print more money to bail them out. This caused the value of the dollar to drop significantly because of an oversupply of dollars in the marketplace.

The oversupply of dollars being printed will at some point lead to an increase in inflation, which is the worst scenario for the economy as people will not have the money to purchase items and that will lead to loss of jobs. You can again see that everything started with government intervention into the free market system.

I wrote, "It behooves every man who values liberty of conscience for him, to resist invasions of it in the case of others." This is a perfect example of giving up liberty because the government wanted to make the case that everyone deserved to own a home.

Q: Why would the banks go along with lowering their credit standards and putting themselves at risk?

Jefferson: First of all, greed took place. They believed that all of the risk was with the federal government, which really means the risk was all with the taxpayer. The government involvement with the banks allowed greed to flourish without the inherent risks that business normally takes and considers when they are making their corporate policies.

The second is they were forced to comply with the government because of threats made by the government. They threaten that if they don't go along with their goals, they can pull their charter thereby putting them out of business. They also can threaten audits by the Federal Reserve, which can cost millions of dollars in actual costs as well as tying up the banks' staff for months.

As I have said before, governments are not benevolent. Given power they become tyrannical. I have spoken often about the nature of government, to grow and seize power, and concerning this I wrote, "The natural progress of things is for liberty to yield and government to gain ground."

The government, regardless of intent, brought upon this country a calamity of huge proportions that would have been avoided if they never became involved in the first place. Look past the intent, look at what result may occur. Government involvement in taking from one to appease another never works in the long run.

Q: What are your feelings about the government investing in other businesses such as the automobile industry?

Jefferson: My feelings are exactly the same. Stay out of business. They claim that if a manufacturer went out of business, it would create massive unemployment so they again take taxpayer money and put it into individual businesses that they deem essential. Is that fair to other businesses? Isn't it still true that growth springs eternal from the ruins of disasters? Don't forests renew after a fire?

Look at history, Sears was the largest retailer and basically collapsed and what happened? New businesses were created to fill the void. The same thing with IBM and K-Mart! Wal-Mart sprang up and someday they will fail as well.

Where is American Motors and Packard? Many automobile manufacturers have come and gone. Entrepreneurs spring up from the ruins of a collapsed company; they start new companies and employ people to work in their new companies. This is the way of commerce.

Look for the real reason that GM as an example was too big to fail, the bailout was to protect the unions. Why would the government be interested in protecting the unions? Votes! Votes mean political power, so they needed to protect its base of power. Why do they allow unions in government jobs? The purpose of the union is to protect their members from unscrupulous employers. With the government, aren't they protected firsthand by all the laws enacted to protect employees? Why should the taxpayer have to pay more than what the marketplace dictates for civil service employees? The reason is that they historically vote as a block for the government that will protect their jobs. This again translates into power for the government. The government as with banking should have no involvement with unions. It can lead to mob rule.

President Ronald Reagan fired all of the air traffic controllers when they went on strike. He correctly stated it was illegal for them to strike and ordered them back to work or be fired. People all over the country said that there would be a massive shutdown of our airways, but President Reagan brought in military personnel to man the flight towers. He also refused to rehire any of the strikers making it clear to all government unions that there would be consequences if they did strike against the government. He was not interested in power; he was interested in maintaining rule of law.

We appear to have very few of these politicians these days. I believe what I said years ago is still applicable, "The government can do something for the people only in proportion as it can do something to the people."

Q: The country is now addressing the issue of health care. Some say it is a Constitutional right, while others say it is not a right. Where do you fall on this issue?

Jefferson: There is no place in the Constitution that says health care is a Constitutional right. The general welfare clause that we discussed earlier certainly does not cover health care. The free market system can provide better health care at a fair price if left alone without all of the government involvement.

Why is the cost so high people ask? Look at the government as the answer to your question. Government got involved when President Franklin Roosevelt, during the Great Depression instituted wage and price controls. The free market's response to this was to find a way to attract employees they needed by offering benefits paid by the company as a way to get around the wage and price controls. This led to a third party paying the cost of health insurance. Since the consumer was no longer paying the cost of medical care directly, they were not concerned with the cost; therefore, the cost grew rapidly. Unintended consequences again for government involvement!

Another cost for health care is lawsuits filed against the medical industry that in many cases are outrages in both their claims and their demands for restitution. With insurance companies paying the damages, juries routinely feel they give the claimant what they want as they don't see any cost to them personally, which is certainly not the case. There is no downside for the attorneys to file frivolous lawsuits.

Why doesn't the government reform this system? It is simple. The American Bar Association is a huge contributor to the political system, so don't bite the hand that feeds you. You could set up an arbitration system where the plaintiff and the defendant would make their case before a legal arbiter who would decide on the facts what is reasonable or not. If the plaintiff or the defendant does not agree to the decision, they would have legal right to take it to court, but then the loser of the case would be responsible for all costs incurred by the court action. There must be some risk incurred by either party in taking the case to court. This would cease frivolous suits almost immediately and still protect everyone's Constitutional rights to a fair trial.

Q: Are there any other ways you feel that health care costs could be controlled?

Jefferson: Get government out of the way and let the free enterprise system work. They have laws now restricting the offering of health insurance across state lines. This does not allow for free competition, and therefore you have higher premiums due to lack of competition. The government should not be involved in curtailing competition.

Why did they enact laws to hamper free enterprise from competing? Simple answer—money! There are huge profits if a company does not have to compete openly. It is much cheaper to fill the coffers of politicians than it is to compete on the open market.

Q: Continuing with the issue of health care, the government says they can provide more care for less cost to the individual than greedy private insurance companies. Do you believe this?

Jefferson: Look at history. When has the government been fiscally responsible? If private business ran their businesses like the government does, there would not be enough prisons to hold all those who would be convicted of fraud and embezzlement. Take programs like Social Security and Medicare. All have been so poorly mismanaged that it is criminal.

If you make decisions like most wise men, based on history, why would you turn your health over to an entity that has failed on every venture in the past? Would you want to choose a surgeon to operate on you when every other patient he has operated on in the past has died? I think not! It is the same as turning health care over to the government. Look at the bills they are writing regarding health care. They are two-thousand pages long, incoherent! They cover everything from health care to building a sewer plant in Alabama. Why the sewer plant you ask? Because it is a bribe to get the politician's vote for the bill that he would never support without the bribe.

James Madison wrote, "It will be of little avail to the people that the laws are made by men of their own choice if the laws be so voluminous that they cannot be read, or so incoherent that they cannot be understood." Do you honestly think that two-thousand-page bills are coherent? Why do they negotiate in the darkness of smoke-filled back rooms rather than out in the open? What do they have to hide? What deals were made with AARP, with AMA, with insurance companies, etc? No one knows as the press and public are kept outside of the dealings.

Patrick Henry wrote on this subject: "The liberties of a people never were, nor ever will be, secure, when the transactions of their rulers may be concealed from them." I think that says it all! The Constitution was written on seventeen pages. There is a hidden reason that a bill has to be two-thousand pages, and hidden agendas are nefarious by nature.

Q: I understand what you are saying, but I don't think you addressed my question of cost?

Jefferson: I apologize, as I stated, there is no history whatsoever that indicates the government could control costs. Let's look at what has to be done to control cost. First you have to have fewer people with access to health care services. How do you accomplish this if you are going to cover everyone? You must reduce births; this is done with an increase in abortions, aborting babies that have birth defects that would require medical care now and in the future. If that doesn't reduce the number of births satisfactorily, then you will have the government dictate the number of children that can be born per family. This is now being done in China with disastrous results as they have a huge percentage of males and not enough females.

At some point you could see a revolution over the issue. Now you must control cost on the other end of the spectrum, which is with the elderly. You will see that the elderly will not get the medical care needed as it is expensive and can run into many years of needed medical care. Someone will make the decision on who gets care and how much the elderly will receive. Stop incoming population, and end the elderly liability as quickly as possible.

You will also see a reduction in tests for all people as that opens the door for expensive medical care. Fewer mammograms and prostate exams will be available as an example. If you don't detect the problem, you don't have to treat it. The last piece you will see is the reduction of research in both treatment and in medicine— the reason again is that if you have the means to detect a medical condition you will be obligated to treat it. New treatments are very expensive. The same holds true for medical prescriptions.

If I sound like a naysayer, you are right. There is *nothing* good that can happen with a government-run health care system. Look at the countries that have national health care, and they all follow what I outlined to you. We will be no different. James Madison wrote, "The essence of Government is power; and power as it must be in human hands, will ever be liable to abuse."

Q: From what I understand, people or states would have the option of opting out of the government plan. Wouldn't this protect the individual?

Jefferson: The system needs everyone to pay into it to be able to offer any services. Private insurance companies with the loss of their client base will no longer have the resources to stay in business; the government will force them out. How can a private company compete with the government that doesn't rely on a profit and when losses are incurred they will just tax the taxpayer?

The government also makes all the rules for which private companies have to comply but the government doesn't. With that type of playing field, do you think any private company could compete and remain profitable? What recourse would you have when the rules are made by the government and enforced by the government? Who would you take your grievances too? We have all heard the phrase, you can't fight city hall. Well what do you then feel about fighting the federal government?

Q: There are environmental concerns with the use of fossil energies, but can we prosper as a nation without the use of these energies?

Jefferson: When alternative energies are available at a reasonable cost and are reliable, the nation will move in that direction. Why is the government forcing people and industries against their will to reduce or eliminate these sources of energy? Do you believe it is purely done for the environment? It is for power, it is a way for redistributing wealth.

The science of global warming is shaky at best, but it is treated as gospel that no one should challenge the data. That goes against the principles of science. In science, you come up with a theory and then must prove that theory, and part of proving the theory is to challenge the theory. To find holes in the theory and then to dispel them!

Why is anyone who challenges the theory of global warming treated as a lunatic, as a person who wants to destroy the environment? Why are they ridiculed and demeaned? It is because there is an agenda. The answer is money and power. Have they made it known what effect these laws can have on possible loss of jobs and income and that this government would be required to give away their wealth to third-world countries? Absolutely not as it would destroy their initiative! This is a means just as national health care to take away your right to wealth and liberty. To form a means of government controlling everything in your life by taking away your personal wealth!

I wrote, "An elective despotism was not the government we fought for, but one which should not only be founded on true free principles. but in which the powers of government would be so divided and balanced among several bodies of magistracy, as that no one could transcend their legal limits without being effectually checked and restrained by others."

Where in the Constitution does it give the federal government the right to restrict the use of natural resources? I also wrote, "It is not only vain, but wicked, in a legislature to frame laws in opposition to the laws of nature, and to arm them with terrors of death. This is truly creating crimes in order to punish them." Another quote of mine I believe is applicable, "Were we directed from Washington when to sow and when to reap, we should soon want bread."

Q: But Mr. Jefferson, isn't government just trying to prevent us from destroying the environment?

Jefferson: That would be assuming that manmade global warming is factual science. I have never heard of consensual science. Have they changed the laws of science to make science anything we wish it to be? If you were in a room of one hundred people and sixty-seven of the hundred said that earth rotated around the moon, would it now be fact, would it now be settled science? Would you base your family wealth on this science? Would you now risk your and your family jobs on this "settled science"? I think not!

On this "settled science" are you now willing to give to the government your wealth so that they can give it to someone else as some politician deems fit? If so, what other liberties do you wish to turn over to what you must believe is an all-knowing and magnanimous body of people? I once said, "We have the greatest opportunities the world has ever seen, as long as we remain honest—which will be as long as we can keep the attention of our people alive. If they once become inattentive to public affairs, you and I, and Congress and Assemblies, judges and governors would all become wolves."

As with all things there can be unintended consequences of actions taken. Some can be positive and some can be negative. The government is controlling the use of waterways in California in order to protect a species of fish. This is driving farmers out of business. This also has the effect of raising prices of agricultural products. Is this something that the people of California want? Certainly not! People who live there locally should be making those decisions, not some bureaucrats two-thousand miles away.

14

National Security: The First Priority of Government

Q: I would like to change topics and address national security. How does the Constitution address the issue of national security and a military?

Jefferson: The Constitution addresses this issue clearly. The Constitution gives specific powers to the Congress under Section 8. They are as follows:

- To declare War, grant Letters of Marque and Reprisal, and make Rules concerning Captures on Land and Water;
- To raise and support Armies, but no Appropriation of Money to that Use shall be for a longer Term than two years;
- To provide and maintain a Navy;
- To make Rules for the Government and Regulation of the land and naval forces;
- To provide for calling forth the Militia to execute the Laws of the Union, suppress Insurrections and repel Invasions;

- To provide for organizing, arming, and disciplining,
  the Militia, and for governing such Part of them as
  may be employed in the Service of the United States,
  reserving to the States respectively, the Appointment of
  the Officers, and the Authority of training the Militia
  according to the discipline prescribed by Congress;
- To exercise exclusive Legislation in all Cases whatsoever,
  over such District (not exceeding ten Miles square) as
  may by Cession of particular States, and the Acceptance
  of Congress, become the Seat of the Government of
  the United States, and to exercise like Authority over all
  Places purchased by the Consent of the Legislature of
  the State in which the Same shall be, for the Erection
  of Forts, Magazines, Arsenals, dock-yards and other
  needful buildings;—And
- To make all laws which shall be necessary and proper
  for carrying into Execution the foregoing Powers, and
  all other Powers vested by this Constitution in the
  Government of the United States, or in any Department
  or Officer thereof.

Benjamin Franklin wrote, "Our security lies, I think, in our growing strength, both in numbers and wealth; that creates an increasing ability of assisting this nation in its wars, which will make us more respectable, thence it will soon be thought proper to treat us not with justice only, but with kindness, and thence we may expect in a few years a total change of measures with regard to us; unless, by neglect of military discipline, we should lose all martial spirit, and our western people become as tame as those in the eastern dominions of Britain, when we may expect the same oppressions; for there is much truth in the Italian saying, 'Make yourselves sheep, and the wolves will eat you.'"

I do not believe that man can walk away from threats and still remain free. Concerning this I wrote, "I have sworn upon the altar of God, eternal hostility against every form of tyranny over the mind of man."

Q: The first power given is the power of the Congress to declare war, yet we have been in many wars that Congress did not approve but did approve funding for the non-declared war. How can this be?

Jefferson: This in my opinion is a clear violation of the Constitution. It is Congress abdicating their responsibility. There should be no commitment of United States armies or naval forces against another country or threat without the declaration of war. It is weakness, the desire not to be held accountable to history that leads Congress not to have a formal declaration of war. It is the way of cowards.

Regarding character I wrote, "In matters of style, swim with the current; in matters of principle, stand like a rock." Korea and Vietnam are two examples of Congress violating the Constitution. They used semantics to avoid declaration of war and the responsibility that goes with declaring war. If there is not a justifiable cause in which to declare war, we should not be sending our men and women in battles to die for anything less than a declared war. They, Congress, in my opinion further violated the Constitution by funding these undeclared wars. Have they no souls? Is there a use of power more important than the survival of this great nation founded on the Constitution? I would like to know the justification for these acts. What justification can there be for sending people to die for a cause that you are not willing to declare those justifications? I have said, "One man with courage is a majority."

President Washington wrote: "War—An act of violence whose object is to constrain the enemy, to accomplish our will." Now if Congress would have believed and followed this, why not declare if we are to repel our enemy for a just cause? It is purely lack of courage. I sometimes believe our politicians are what Benjamin Franklin wrote, "Trickery and treachery are the practices of fools that have not the wits enough to be honest."

Are the politicians so naive that they think we can so easily be deceived or that so frail that we cannot bear the truth? Patrick Henry wrote: "We are apt to shut our eyes against a painful truth … For my part, I am willing to know the whole truth; to know the worst; and to provide for it." Maybe Congress should read more from Patrick Henry.

Q: But there could be times that we need a call to arms to honor a treaty or in our national security but Congress won't declare war. What do we do in those situations?

Jefferson: The answer is in the Constitution: the country does not go to war. If you cannot get Congress to authorize war, the country cannot go to war. I have said, "I have seen enough of one war never to wish to see another." If they don't believe the country should go to war for any reason, the country cannot go. If it is just they don't want to vote for war for political fears, the country still cannot commit to war, and in my opinion they should be thrown out of office for not acting in our country's best interest.

We have committed thousands of young men and women over the last fifty years or so to war with thousands of them being killed without a declaration of war. Not only is it unconstitutional, it is an act of cowardice.

Q: But what about the War on Terror? Is that not a declared war? It is not against a country but was meant to take action to insure the safety of this country. What do you do about a declaration of war when there is no specific country in which to declare war on?

Jefferson: We were dealing with the same issue in my time. In 1786 John Adams and I wrote this: "History records them as the Barbary Pirates. In fact they were blackmailing terrorists, hiding behind a self-serving interpretation of their Islamic faith by embracing select tracts and ignoring others. Borrowing from the Christian Crusades of centuries past, they used history as a mandate for doing the western world one better. The quisling European powers had been buying them off for years. We took the liberty to make some inquires concerning the Grounds of their pretensions to make war upon a Nation who had done them no injury, and observed that we considered all mankind as our friends who had done us no wrong, nor had given us any provocation. The ambassador answered us that it was founded on the laws of their Koran, that all nations who should not have acknowledged their authority were sinners, that it was their right and duty to make war upon them wherever they could be found, and to make slaves of all they could take as prisoners, and that every Musselman who should be slain in battle was sure to go to Paradise."

I wanted a military solution back then. Decades of Europeans attempting to bribe them to gain peace was an abject failure. There was no stomach for declaring war so war was not waged. By looking at the situation this country is in today validates my judgment back then. The terrorists have not changed in the last two centuries and will not change in the next no matter how hard we try to appease or justify their actions. The only lawful way is to declare war on these Islamic terrorists.

Q: But wouldn't that declaration of war bring the whole Islamic religion against us? What about world opinion?

Jefferson: Margaret Thatcher once said that leadership is not compromise. You must stand for the rule of law, Natural Law! That every man has rights that are given to him by the Almighty and these cannot be allowed to be taken away from fear of public opinion or by fear of another's religion.

In the 1700s America paid out $990,000 in blackmail to supposedly give us peace from the Algerians. That was back when our total national revenues were just $7 million. We paid out a seventh of our wealth in blackmail and what did we gain from this act of cowardice? We gained nothing and gave them the power to continue their acts of terror across the world.

There have always been great callings to rid the world of evil and this is no different. Do you want to live in fear and be enslaved or do you wish to live as free men? That is the simple question with very hard answers to deal with. William Eaton, a U.S. Counsel wrote in 1799, "There is but one language which can be held to these people, and this is terror."

Most of the world does not enjoy freedom as Americans have enjoyed, hence they do not have the will to fight for something they don't enjoy. You ask if we would be declaring war on the Islamic religion. Only to the sect that advocates terror on others, but let it be known that if they condone terror by looking the other way and harboring them for the purpose of giving them a safe place to prepare for their acts of terror that they will be held as responsible as the one that commits their acts of terror.

Q: What do you think would help us with our war against Islamic terrorism besides military action?

Jefferson: We must eliminate political correctness. You cannot win any war unless all citizens understand the threat that faces us and what the consequences are if we do not face up to our enemies. You cannot sugar coat your enemies or their ability to destroy your freedom and lives. Only when the people are informed can they make the proper decisions regarding their safety.

I wrote, "Whenever the people are well-informed, they can be trusted with their own government; whenever things get so wrong as to attract their notice, they may be relied upon to set them to rights." What I am saying is that when informed, the people I believe will take the right path. When you have political correctness, you lose the ability to communicate. Do politicians believe you are not strong enough to know the truth or are they interested in protecting themselves? The people need to have information given to them in clean, clear terms. I do not fear knowledge and do not believe that the people of this country do either.

Regarding the subject of having the people informed, I stated, "If a nation expects to be ignorant and free, in a state of civilization, it expects what never was and never will be."

Q: Many might take what you view as war mongering? How would you answer that charge?

Jefferson: President Washington said, "To be prepared for war is one of the most effectual means of preserving peace." Freedom comes with a price. I abhor war as any sane man would do, but history will tell you that if you will not stand up and fight for your freedom, you shall soon lose it.

I have never advocated war for gain for this country, only to preserve our autonomy, to preserve our liberty for us and our sons and daughters. Samuel Adams wrote, "The liberties of our country, the freedom of our civil Constitution are worth defending at all hazards." To expand further on my beliefs, I turn to what John Adams said, "People and nations are forged in the fires of Adversity. Whenever the standard of freedom and independence has been or shall be unfurled, there will be America's heart, her benedictions and prayers, but she goes not abroad in search of monsters to destroy. She is well-wisher to the freedom and independence of all. She is the champion and vindicator of her own will."

I think that makes it clear that I do not wish war for any reason other than liberty. I agree with Thomas Paine when he said, "Those who expect to reap the blessings of freedom, must, like men, undergo the fatigues of supporting it." I also refer to Benjamin Franklin who said, "They that can give up essential liberty to purchase a little temporary safety, deserve neither liberty nor safety."

You must maintain a force that protects the country. Weak countries are always going to be threatened by a stronger nation. I once said, "A coward is much more exposed to quarrels than a man of spirit." This does not give any nation the right to use that force but to serve as a warning to others that there can be grave repercussions if our sovereignty is threatened. You have more of an opportunity for peace with a strong nation versus having peace with the hope that no one will ever threaten you.

President Washington said, "To be prepared for war is one of the most effectual means of preserving peace."

Q: How do treaties with other nations affect our national security?

Jefferson: President Washington wrote concerning relationships with other countries that I believe is applicable to your question: "In the execution of a plan nothing is more essential than that permanent, inveterate antipathies against particular nations and passionate attachments for others should be excluded, and that in place of them just and amicable feelings toward all should be cultivated. The nation which indulges toward another a habitual hatred or a habitual fondness is in some degree a slave. It is a slave to its animosity or to its affection, either of which is sufficient to lead it astray from its duty and its interest."

Treaties with other countries should be kept to an absolute minimum, and they should have a specific timetable for renewal of that treaty. Treaties that do not have an equal benefit to both parties should not be entered into. I once stated, "Friendship with all … alliances with none." Many countries would like to enter into a treaty with a military power so that they feel they are protected from outside forces without having to expend their own resources for that end.

I believe NATO is such a treaty with a group of nations that pledge to defend each other. The truth of it is that the United States pays the bulk of the cost for the defense of the organization and when there have been times that force was called upon and it was not handled equally. The United States paid the bulk of the financial costs as well as military forces. A great example of this was the war in the Balkans, which a great threat to Europe, but yet it was this country that spent its treasury and lives in that conflict. Why is it in our best interest to have such treaties when the real benefit is to others and not this country?

Ronald Reagan wrote, "History teaches that war begins when governments believe the price of aggression is cheap." They must be equal partners in all aspects, not just signers of the treaties. Treaties are usually written to cover a long period of time. Time changes countries' policies and goals. This is especially true of countries that do not have sound governments in place. You can be making commitments to countries that no longer share your views. You put the nation's soldiers and treasure at risk for goals that are contrary to our national interest.

Q: How can energy policies put our country at risk?

Jefferson: Look no further than the Middle East for an answer to your question. The government has curtailed our use of energy in many forms. A country's industry and wealth are dependent upon energy. With the restrictions on use and exploration of energy, the country and industry have to go to outside sources to get the energy they need.

Recent history shows that the country has entered into agreements to purchase oil from many nations including the Middle East. Most of these countries are run by dictators, despots, and tyrants. The selling of oil to the United States has made them wealthy beyond most people's comprehension. They can dictate prices which affect our economy and job creation. They have been involved with many terrorist groups. Saudi Arabia has done much of the financing of Muslim extremists. They have done this to buy off violence from these extremists, but it allows these terrorists to have the financial means to plan and carry out attacks against the U.S. Since we are dependent on their oil for our needs, we are at their mercy and cannot put the proper pressure on the country to stop this funding of terrorists.

You cannot get into bed with any country that does not share the basic values of human rights. Not respecting human rights tells you immediately that they cannot be a long-term business partner. If we had been creating and using more of our own energy, we would not be financing the same terrorists that have vowed to destroy this great nation.

The government says that we must protect the environment, which I don't believe they are doing, but by doing so they are exposing the country to war. You don't have to be a Harvard-educated person to see the fallacy in this plan. The first role of government is to protect its citizens, not endanger them and the future of the country on an environmental policy.

Patrick Henry wrote the following, "Guard with jealous attention the public liberty. Suspect every one who approaches that jewel. Unfortunately, nothing will preserve it but downright force. Whenever you give up that force, you are ruined."

Q: This country cannot be an isolationist country; we need to trade and share information with other countries. How do we do this and still be able to protect the country?

Jefferson: First, if we do what is necessary at home to become as self-sufficient as possible, we take away our dependency on other countries. That is not being an isolationist; it is being prudent and responsible. This way we can deal from a position of strength rather that weakness. We have the ability to quit doing business with any country that we feel is not acting in a manner that we feel is compatible to our national interests.

In the example of Saudi Arabia that we spoke of earlier, we would be able to cut off trade with them thereby having a huge impact on their country without impacting ours. This would be a huge amount of pressure being borne by them to stop funding and support of terrorists. They would have to develop their own forces to deal with the threat of Muslim extremists rather than paying them off for non-violence against them. That alone would put our country in a much safer position. This policy should be directed to all countries that we wish to trade with, but the first requisite is that we never become dependent on a foreign entity.

Q: What are your thoughts on nuclear disarmament? Would the world be safer if all countries would eliminate nuclear arms?

Jefferson: That is a fantasy that some entertain. You cannot put the genie back into the bottle. If the major powers disarmed, do you honestly think that rogue nations such as Iran and North Korea are going to eliminate their quest for nuclear arms? Absolutely not! We disarm and we will be at risk because we will not have adequate defenses to protect ourselves.

In World War II we developed the nuclear bomb before the Germans who were also working on developing their own. Can you imagine what the world would look like today if they had been successful in beating the United States in creating this weapon? What did the United States do with this weapon? We ended the war! The United States did not look for world domination; we did not wish to gain control of Japan or Europe! No, what we desired was peace, so we used this massive weapon to bring an end to a war that was killing millions of people and would continue killing millions of people. There was no intent to use this weapon for nefarious means, and history bears this out. We can thank the good Lord for watching over us and the world in that period of time as I believe, without his guidance, evil could have ruled the world.

The Soviet Union had a massive military build-up that threatened not only us but all of Europe. Did President Reagan disarm in hope that the Soviets would disarm as well? No, he built up our forces so that the Soviet Union knew that any action against this country would be retaliated against in such a powerful manner that the Soviet Union would be destroyed. That strength was what brought the Soviets to the bargaining table to discuss ways that the countries could benefit mutually. This has given the country peace with a major adversary that could never have been achieved any way other than through strength.

Alexander Hamilton wrote in the Federalist Papers: "Let us recollect that peace or war will not always be left to our option; that however moderate or unambitious we may be, we cannot count upon the moderation, or hope to extinguish the ambition of others."

Q: The United Nations calls for disarmament treaties, doesn't that tell us that the world wants a nuclear-free planet?

Jefferson: The United Nations is not interested in the self-protection of the United States. Let's look at the membership of the United Nations. Two-thirds of the nations in the United Nations are countries run by dictators, warlords, and tyrants. We are to follow the direction laid out by these types of countries? They want us to disarm, which would make them more powerful because they would have less to fear in the way of reprisals when they go about their business of killing people and violating their rights or the rights of other countries. They would not be in favor of disarmament if they had nuclear weapons.

As I pointed out, the world has nothing to fear from the United States having nuclear weapons. We have had them for more than half a century, and we have never used that power to take over any other country. In fact the case has been made that we have used that potential power to protect individual freedom in other countries. Why is Europe still free? Do we honestly think that the Soviet Union had no intentions of invading and controlling all of Europe? History points out clearly that it was the United States and its military force that kept Europe free.

George Washington wrote concerning war: "My first wish is to see this plague of mankind, war, banished from the earth." He also understood the best way to avoid war is through strength.

Samuel Adams summed up what I believe is the mantra we should follow concerning force, "The liberties of our country, the freedom of our civil Constitution, are worth defending at all hazards; and it is our duty to defend them against all attacks. We have received them as a fair inheritance from our worthy ancestors: they purchased them for us with toil and danger and expense of treasure and blood, and transmitted them to us with care and diligence. It will bring an everlasting mark of infamy on the present generation. Enlightened as it is, if we should suffer them to be wrested from us by violence without a struggle, or to be cheated out of them by the artifices of false and designing men."

I would like to add regarding the United Nations, I view this body as an institution that does not have the United States in its best interest and therefore we should withdraw from it. This "government institution" is like all government institutions, it has an insatiable thirst for expansion of power. I believe the goal of the United Nations is to become the world government, which would be the most egregious thing I can imagine for this country and the world as a whole.

Regarding the Untied Nations and a world government, I once wrote, "The way to have safe government is not to trust it all to the one, but to divide it among the many, distributing to everyone exactly the functions in which he is competent." I view the United Nations as a threat to everyone's liberty, not just in this country but a threat to every man's liberty.

Q: You appear to be saying that you do not have faith in the United Nations, is that true?

Jefferson: I believe it is an immoral body of government with no legal basis for any governing. It is immoral as it has done nothing to stop genocide when it occurs; it has always been left up to the United States. Do you believe a man would fight for this global body rather than that of his own country? Has the United Nations educated the world? Stopped poverty? Given freedom to any of its member nations that are run by despots, dictators, and thugs? The answer is no. It is an impotent body that only gives a means for barbarian countries to voice their hate for freedom and liberty. It is a body of government with no teeth.

Q: If we don't follow a path of disarmament, won't nuclear weapons continue to proliferate until no one is safe?

Jefferson: The world is not a safe place. As we discussed, would you feel safer without weapons to defend yourself while others are armed? We have to continue to look for ways that would make nuclear weapons obsolete. The Strategic Defense Initiative that was started by President Reagan brought scorn from his skeptics but yet the fear of a defense shield brought the Soviet Union to the bargaining table. We must look for defense systems that would protect our country and that is the only way that I see that the non-proliferation of nuclear weapons would occur. Make them less effective. This might seem like a fantasy but so was radio, microwaves, and space travel. We must seek out answers, there are always solutions.

Q: What role does our national debt play in our national security?

Jefferson: It plays a major role in our national security both internally and externally. I covered earlier how it affects us internally so will just address the issue of external.

When we cannot pay our creditors such as Japan, Saudi Arabia, and others, they can hold us hostage. We cannot deal with them fairly and must bow to their demands for fear that they would call in our notes and we would be unable to pay. Defaulting on these notes would destroy our currency and creditability throughout the world.

Look at what happened when China was found to be selling us toys that were painted using lead that can lead to illness or death. We asked them to change their system of painting and we did little else. If an American company did that, there would have been severe penalties to that company, which might have led to the closing of the company. Did we investigate other Chinese companies as we should have to ensure all the products coming into our country meet our safety standards? No we did not! Why? For fear that they could bring retribution to us because of our debt to them. That is not in the best interests of the American people.

Can we deal with them from a position of strength with our concerns with nuclear proliferation with North Korea or Iran? No, we again must bend to their will. It is just as much concern to our long-term sovereignty as their nuclear weapons.

15

Summary: What Direction Will America Take?

As Jefferson has told us, America has faced crossroads in the past. We have had Americans fight Americans during the Civil War—a war that tore at the core the principles of America. Do all men have the right to be free? Would America stand the moral test of equality and justice or would they become just another country whose leaders decide who has rights and liberties and who does not? America lost over 620,000 men and women during the Civil War. That is more deaths than the Revolutionary War, The War of 1812, Mexican American War, Spanish American War, World War I, World War II, Korean War, and the Vietnam combined.

Why was America willing to pay such a price in blood of their children? Because a country must be moral if it is to survive! It must be willing to fight for what is right or the country will collapse into the ash heaps of history just as so many countries in the past have done.

We had the Great Depression, which caused massive unemployment and fear for our future. We did not have unemployment insurance for people to rely upon; they had to rely on each other, on family, friends, community, and on their faith and churches. What is amazing is that during these tough times, crime went down not up as most people would assume. Why? Because people of character in tough times band together to survive. America is home to people of character, make no doubt about it. People are individuals, not masses, and individuals found ways to make it through the painful economic times. They had pride in themselves, not dependency on a government entity.

In World War II we were faced with powers in Germany, Japan, and Italy that wanted world domination. They were out to eliminate freedom; they wanted to rule the world as they believed, not as the people believed. They believed in eugenics, believed in a superior race. Many Americans including those in government believed it was Europe's problem; we were separated by massive oceans, why should we join the fight? America stood up for what is right and just, what is moral.

During the Cold War, the Soviet Union was expanding communism, imposing their will upon other nations and its people. If it were not for the United States they would have swept across Europe and there was no one to stop them. The United States was the only force standing in the way of the Soviet Union, and stand in their way we did. Anyone who thinks the spreading of communism was a good thing should look at East Germany and West Germany. The Soviets had to build a wall with barbed wire and armed guards to keep people from fleeing to West Germany. There were no people from West Germany trying to cross the wall into East Germany. Why was the wall necessary? Because people desired freedom and would try to escape tyranny to achieve it. President John Kennedy started an airlift of supplies to the people of West Berlin when the Soviet Union formed a blockade in an attempt to starve out the people of West Berlin so that they would surrender and become part of the Soviet Empire.

Years later, President Ronald Reagan challenged the Soviets publicly to "tear down this wall." He risked a military confrontation with the Soviets in order to gain freedom for the people of Germany.

Americans have fought many wars yet we do not seek to gain from the spoils of victory. We do not claim their land, resources, or their wealth. When the wars have ended, we go home to our families and even help rebuild the nations of those that fought us. Paraphrasing General Colin Powell, all we have asked is for a small plot of land in which to bury our dead.

When there are world disasters from earthquakes, flooding, hurricanes, droughts, or other natural disasters, who does the world turn to? It is always the United States. There are many wealthy countries in the world, but the help they offer is minimal or nonexistent and the reason is that those countries are not based on natural law and morality. We need to know, while there have been mistakes made by this country, this country has a truly great history and the world would be a much poorer place if the United States had never been founded.

This country is based upon free men who will reap the rewards of their efforts. This has brought the highest standard of living known to man. That system is called the free market system—a system of limited government and massive freedoms. It created an environment that has produced some of the world's greatest achievements. We have seen miracles in medicine that have eradicated diseases such as polio and leprosy and increased life expectancy by 25 percent. Inventions have changed the world: the automobile, airplanes, electricity, and the telephone.

Does anyone honestly think this country could have achieved these innovations without a free market system? Do we think with a government-controlled environment we would be the nation that we are now? If so, look at history and find a socialist, communist, or Marxist country that has achievements that have benefited man the way that this country has. Look at those nations. Have they defended other nations or peoples when there has been an attack on those peoples rights or lives?

The contribution by Americans to the world is limitless, and we have asked for nothing in return except to allow those that achieve these things to keep the fruits of their labor. Now we have some who say take from those who have achieved and give to those who do not, and they believe that our country will continue to prosper.

We now are faced with another financial crisis—one of our own making. One that was created by government mandates, over reaching into the rights of states and individuals. This was not done over five or ten years but over the last one hundred years, like a drip of water, eroding the surface so slowly that we didn't notice until the damage was massive.

We must now ask the question: Do Americans still love liberty and freedom or are they willing to give up their freedom for a temporary sense of security? I say temporary because history shows us quite clearly that there is no utopia where the hard-working individual will continue to work to take care of those who don't.

- Do they believe that they as individuals must have control of their own destiny or do they believe a magnanimous government will take care of their future?
- Do they believe we are a nation formed on natural law or do we believe in manmade laws that can change over time by the whims of a government?
- Are we naïve enough to think that governments of now and in the future will be moral and always have the best interests of its people at heart?

Man is flawed by nature and must strive to overcome these flaws, and history shows us that men with power must be controlled by the people, and not have the power to control the people. People have said that times are different than they were in the 1700s, scientifically that is correct, but human nature has not changed over the years. Government is manmade and is still controlled by men—individuals with the same flaws as in the past.

What must we do to remain free and continue our prosperity? We must take back the control of our lives and not allow the government to have that control. Our destiny is ours, not left to someone else or some other entity. How do we do that?

We do it by being involved in our communities, by speaking out and holding our leaders accountable to the Constitution. It starts with local government and our schools. We must elect people on the local level who espouse our values. They are the people that our state and national leaders elected from. When we do not become involved locally, the wrong people gain power, and we are responsible for their decisions.

In the schools we must demand excellence; we cannot continue to lower the bar and expect that our children will grow up to be achievers in society. Locally you must set the expectations for your children, not let the state or federal government set them. Teachers must be held accountable, they must teach to the local community standards, or they must be fired. There can be no room for teachers who do not have the skills or the will to teach our children the academics that they will need to be successful in society. We must demand that the basics of math, science, reading, writing, and history be taught. Make sure that the Constitution is taught in school and what natural law is and why it was the foundation of our nation.

When a community decides that too much teaching time is being taken for frivolous subjects, they must have those removed, and the state and federal governments should not be able to impose their will in these matters. Eliminate the federal government from involvement in education; eliminate taxes being sent to the federal government for education. On average, for every dollar of federal taxpayer money that is sent to the federal government and earmarked for education, only twenty-six cents comes back to the state. It makes no fiscal sense for this to continue. It is a waste of taxpayer dollars, and there is no way that they can understand what the local school curriculum or standards should be.

We should abolish the present tax system. It is unfair and so complex even tax attorneys do not understand it. We should replace it with a flat tax or a national sales tax but not both. Either one is simple and easy to forecast future collections. It would eliminate massive waste and fraud in the system. Everyone would have a stake in our country and in how we spend our money. No one would be exempt from taxes. Being simple, it would make it very difficult for government to raise taxes as everyone would see the increase immediately. This is a way to put power back in the hands of the people.

We need to hold all government officials accountable. If they do not follow the Constitution, they must be removed. They take an oath to support the Constitution, so if they don't support the Constitution or try to change it without the process of amendments, they must be removed from office. If judges make laws, they must be removed. Demand that they be impeached!

The Constitution is not a living breathing document, it is *law*. Why should you be required to obey any law if politicians do not follow the law that they take an oath to uphold? The first step in holding government accountable is to be informed and to question with boldness their words and deeds. Be aware of the intent behind the words. When you hear the word *fairness* or *social justice*, run from the issue and do everything possible to eliminate the issue; they are code words for government control. Fairness and social justice were terms used to make socialism or Marxism palatable to the public.

Look at Hitler and Stalin; these words were used extensively in their rise to power. They are words used to have government be able to determine equality of outcome versus equality of opportunity. The Constitution was never written to guarantee equality of outcome, as it is impossible to do without tyranny. Examples of fairness being used is in wage controls, limitation on what some individuals can earn just because someone in the government thinks it is excessive. Taking money from the wealthy and giving to the poor is another fairness term when it is wealth redistribution, which has never worked in any society. The Constitution forbids redistribution of wealth because it destroys society by taking away man's natural ambition and creates dependency.

Fairness in education is another way of grading on a curve rather than by knowledge. You must have standards that must be reached; if no one reaches that standard, the highest failure is not acceptable.

Fairness in the media such as radio, television, print media, and the Internet must never be allowed to happen. It is a deceiving way for the government to tell you what information you are to receive.

Fairness in medical care is another way government can control our lives. They can decide who is born, who is productive, and who is worth the medical care. That is none of government's business and leads to more abortions and euthanasia. You will also see a massive reduction in medical research because research extends life and that leads to long-term medical care being required; you then become a liability to the government. Look at countries with government health care and you see disasters. The best way I can advise you to be on the alert for government intrusion is when they are telling you equality of result is the goal over equality of opportunity.

We must demand from our government officials what we demand from ourselves. Accountability! They have become lords and nobles, and we have done nothing to rein them in. Their wages have gone up to where it is approximately four times a Congressman's wages compared to the civilian workplace. Salary increases should never exceed the cost of living, and they should be required to pay into the Social Security system like all other citizens of this country. Eliminate their pension plan. We should do nothing that encourages them to making Congress a career. The Founding Fathers expressed their desire to keep wages minimal so that they would want to return to civilian life and not make serving in Congress a lifelong career. Term limits must be considered. It worked for the President and it can work in Congress.

They are not accountable for personal expenses. We have Congressmen flying on military jets at enormous expense with no oversight. There is no reason that they cannot fly commercially. Overseas trips should have oversight approval. They take trips and bring family along at our expense. Why is this allowed? The average Congressman spends over $10,000 a year on bottled water. Are there no faucets in Washington? If they desire bottled water for themselves and guests, they can pay for it themselves. Some might say it's ridiculous discussing water but you have to send the message that there is no free ride. They must answer to the people for every dollar spent.

There has to be an oversight with the President as well. The President needs for security purposes to have private flights, but there must be some budget submitted annually for trips, entertaining, etc. There is no reason that millions and millions of dollars are spent on travel and entertaining with no oversight whatsoever by anyone.

We must demand that our leaders and executives are law-abiding people. They must obey the laws of the land just as every citizen must do. If they do not pay their taxes, they should not be considered for office. If they perjure themselves, they must be removed. No double standards can be tolerated.

We must curtail presidential power. The Constitution outlines clearly the President's responsibilities and the limitations of power. We must curtail presidential edicts. Laws are made by Congress and overseen by Congress, and they are not made by any President and are not to be overseen by a President. We must ask why Congress has given up their Constitutional power. George Washington was being considered for being made a king, but he refused and believed it to be despicable. It was then and is still despicable under any name.

Social Security must be made solvent. We must have a minimum of a three-year freeze on Social Security payments. No one wants to reduce Social Security payments, but everyone including the elderly must be willing to do their part to solve this problem. The young must be given the option of putting a percentage of their Social Security payments into the private sector. This will reduce our long-term exposure and also generate billions of dollars for the private sector, which in turn will create jobs. Any future monies collected by Social Security must be kept out of the general fund and used solely for Social Security benefits.

We cannot have an ever expanding government workforce. Pensions for these workers must be reduced. We cannot afford to have a civil servant work for twenty-five years and then draw 90 percent of their wages for the next thirty years plus benefits. This includes local fire and police forces. You start by freezing wages for three years of all civil service employees and freeze any hiring. As people retire or leave they must not be replaced. Departments must shift workloads to accommodate the loss of workers. The civilian workforce goes through this process all the time to remain profitable. Why can't we ask the same from our government workforce? This is the easiest and least painful way of reducing government employees.

Look at what is happening to California. They have over promised and over taxed its people to the point that they are near collapse. They have failed to control its borders and have allowed unfettered immigration. They have increased civil service employees and those dependant on welfare assistance and it has come home to roost. The wealthy are fleeing California for states that are more accommodating. This causes a huge loss in revenues for the state and yet they want to increase taxes more. California is what will happen to our nation without restraints.

We must have the General Accounting Office go through every dollar spent on government programs and recommend the keeping or closing of each program. We cannot pay for rural airports where there are not enough people who use the service to support the service. We can't subsidize trains if there are not enough passengers to make them profitable. We can no longer subsidize anything that should be a market-based function. There is no need for government unions. The purpose of unions if to protect its workers from abuse. The laws guarantee freedom from abuse and they work for the government. Get government out of the private sector. There is no free ride, and they are only offered as silent bribes to increase the power of government.

Return the rights to the states. It is the individual states that must oversee its citizens, not the federal government unless a state is violating federal law. The states are much closer to the wants and needs of the people and can meet those needs much more fiscally responsibly than a large foreign entity. We want the states to compete with other states on education, taxes, employment, and resources. This makes for a healthy nation. We want the citizen to have the opportunity to move to another state if their own state becomes overbearing or onerous to their future. This benefits all citizens and provides competition among the states with little federal involvement. The states must not accept unfunded mandates from the federal government. They are sovereign states. If the government does not return the rights to the states, I believe they should consider the Tenth Amendment.

We must control our borders. Immigration is desirable, but it must be lawful and controlled. All people seeking to come to this country must conform to the laws of this country. If you come illegally, you have already failed the first standard. All people seeking to make this country their home must speak English and must show that they can provide for themselves and their family. All measures necessary must be taken to secure our borders. Immigration control is vital to our national security and our future as a nation.

National security is the first priority of any government. First and foremost, no wars, ever, without a formal declaration of war and approved by Congress. Once war is declared, the President is the Commander in Chief. He makes final decisions on goals and objectives and has the military carry them out. No Constitutional rights to enemy combatants.

Treaties entered into by this country must be few in number and have a clear benefit to this nation.

Part of our national security is energy. States have the rights to energy reserves and production within their boundaries. Offshore resources are controlled by the federal government. We must not be dependent on others for our energy as it weakens our ability to defend ourselves. Government should not subsidize any type of energy regardless of whether it's *clean* energy or not. If the government gets out of the way of the private sector, the private sector will develop the energies that people want and need.

Finally, follow the Constitution. It will lead this country to prosperity while protecting the rights and liberties of all citizens. Equality of opportunity is always the goal, not equality of results. This is the greatest country on earth and can continue to be if we follow the roadmap laid out for us and if we can prevent the intrusion of government into our lives that the Founding Fathers warned us about.

Remain vigilant and hold all of the politicians, local or federal, accountable, and we and our children will live long, prosperous, and free lives as guaranteed under natural law. This was and can continue to be the greatest country on earth, past and future. It will take each individual's commitment to remaining free and to be constantly aware of changes and mandates made by government. Demand the government obey the Constitution and allow every man and woman the right to succeed and fail.

God bless you and God bless America.

Reference Copies

The Declaration of Independence

When, in the course of human events, it becomes necessary for one people to dissolve the political bonds which have connected them with another, and to assume among the powers of the earth, the separate and equal station to which the laws of nature and of nature's God entitle them, a decent respect to the opinions of mankind requires that they should declare the causes which impel them to the separation.

We hold these truths to be self-evident, that all men are created equal, that they are endowed by their Creator with certain unalienable rights, that among these are life, liberty and the pursuit of happiness. That to secure these rights, governments are instituted among men, deriving their just powers from the consent of the governed. That whenever any form of government becomes destructive to these ends, it is the right of the people to alter or to abolish it, and to institute new government, laying its foundation on such principles and organizing its powers in such form, as to them shall seem most likely to effect their safety and happiness. Prudence, indeed, will dictate that governments long established should not be changed for light and transient causes; and accordingly all experience hath shown that mankind are more disposed to suffer, while evils are sufferable, than to right themselves by abolishing the forms to which they are accustomed. But when a long train of abuses and usurpations, pursuing invariably the same object evinces a design to reduce them under absolute despotism, it is their right, it is their duty, to throw off such government, and to provide new guards for their future security. —Such has been the patient sufferance of these colonies; and such is now the necessity which constrains them to alter their former systems of government. The history of the present King of Great Britain is a history of repeated injuries and usurpations, all having in direct object the establishment of an absolute tyranny over these states. To prove this, let facts be submitted to a candid world.

He has refused his assent to laws, the most wholesome and necessary for the public good.

He has forbidden his governors to pass laws of immediate and pressing importance, unless suspended in their operation till his assent should be obtained; and when so suspended, he has utterly neglected to attend to them.

He has refused to pass other laws for the accommodation of large districts of people, unless those people would relinquish the right of representation in the legislature, a right inestimable to them and formidable to tyrants only.

He has called together legislative bodies at places unusual, uncomfortable, and distant from the depository of their public records, for the sole purpose of fatiguing them into compliance with his measures.

He has dissolved representative houses repeatedly, for opposing with manly firmness his invasions on the rights of the people.

He has refused for a long time, after such dissolutions, to cause others to be elected; whereby the legislative powers, incapable of annihilation, have returned to the people at large for their exercise; the state remaining in the meantime exposed to all the dangers of invasion from without, and convulsions within.

He has endeavored to prevent the population of these states; for that purpose obstructing the laws for naturalization of foreigners; refusing to pass others to encourage their migration hither, and raising the conditions of new appropriations of lands.

He has obstructed the administration of justice, by refusing his assent to laws for establishing judiciary powers.

He has made judges dependent on his will alone, for the tenure of their offices, and the amount and payment of their salaries.

He has erected a multitude of new offices, and sent hither swarms of officers to harass our people, and eat out their substance.

He has kept among us, in times of peace, standing armies without the consent of our legislature.

He has affected to render the military independent of and superior to civil power.

He has combined with others to subject us to a jurisdiction foreign to our constitution, and unacknowledged by our laws; giving his assent to their acts of pretended legislation:

For quartering large bodies of armed troops among us:

For protecting them, by mock trial, from punishment for any murders which they should commit on the inhabitants of these states:

For cutting off our trade with all parts of the world:

For imposing taxes on us without our consent:

For depriving us in many cases, of the benefits of trial by jury:

For transporting us beyond seas to be tried for pretended offenses:

For abolishing the free system of English laws in a neighboring province, establishing therein an arbitrary government, and enlarging its boundaries so as to render it at once an example and fit instrument for introducing the same absolute rule in these colonies:

For taking away our charters, abolishing our most valuable laws, and altering fundamentally the forms of our governments:

For suspending our own legislatures, and declaring themselves invested with power to legislate for us in all cases whatsoever.

He has abdicated government here, by declaring us out of his protection and waging war against us.

He has plundered our seas, ravaged our coasts, burned our towns, and destroyed the lives of our people.

He is at this time transporting large armies of foreign mercenaries to complete the works of death, desolation and tyranny, already begun with circumstances of cruelty and perfidy scarcely paralleled in the most barbarous ages, and totally unworthy the head of a civilized nation.

He has constrained our fellow citizens taken captive on the high seas to bear arms against their country, to become the executioners of their friends and brethren, or to fall themselves by their hands.

He has excited domestic insurrections amongst us, and has endeavored to bring on the inhabitants of our frontiers, the merciless Indian savages, whose known rule of warfare, is undistinguished destruction of all ages, sexes and conditions.

In every stage of these oppressions we have petitioned for redress in the most humble terms: our repeated petitions have been answered only by repeated injury. A prince, whose character is thus marked by every act which may define a tyrant, is unfit to be the ruler of a free people.

Nor have we been wanting in attention to our British brethren. We have warned them from time to time of attempts by their legislature to extend an unwarrantable jurisdiction over us. We have reminded them of the circumstances of our emigration and settlement here. We have appealed to their native justice and magnanimity, and we have conjured them by the ties of our common kindred to disavow these usurpations, which, would inevitably interrupt our connections and correspondence. They too have been deaf to the voice of justice and of consanguinity. We must, therefore, acquiesce in the necessity, which denounces our separation, and hold them, as we hold the rest of mankind, enemies in war, in peace friends.

We, therefore, the representatives of the United States of America, in General Congress, assembled, appealing to the Supreme

Judge of the world for the rectitude of our intentions, do, in the name, and by the authority of the good people of these colonies, solemnly publish and declare, that these united colonies are, and of right ought to be free and independent states; that they are absolved from all allegiance to the British Crown, and that all political connection between them and the state of Great Britain, is and ought to be totally dissolved; and that as free and independent states, they have full power to levy war, conclude peace, contract alliances, establish commerce, and to do all other acts and things which independent states may of right do. And for the support of this declaration, with a firm reliance on the protection of Divine Providence, we mutually pledge to each other our lives, our fortunes and our sacred honor.

The Constitution of the United States of America

We the People of the United States, in Order to form a more perfect Union, establish Justice, insure domestic Tranquility, provide for the common defence, promote the general Welfare, and secure the Blessings of Liberty to ourselves and our Posterity, do ordain and establish this Constitution for the United States of America.

Article. I.

Section. 1.

All legislative Powers herein granted shall be vested in a Congress of the United States, which shall consist of a Senate and House of Representatives.

Section. 2.

The House of Representatives shall be composed of Members chosen every second Year by the People of the several States, and the Electors in each State shall have the Qualifications requisite for Electors of the most numerous Branch of the State Legislature.

No Person shall be a Representative who shall not have attained to the Age of twenty five Years, and been seven Years a Citizen of the United States, and who shall not, when elected, be an Inhabitant of that State in which he shall be chosen.

Representatives and direct Taxes shall be apportioned among the several States which may be included within this Union, according to their respective Numbers, which shall be determined by adding to the whole Number of free Persons, including those bound to Service for a Term of Years, and excluding Indians not taxed, three fifths of all other Persons. The actual Enumeration shall be made within three Years after the first Meeting of the Congress of the United States, and within every subsequent Term of ten Years, in such Manner as they shall by Law direct. The Number of Representatives shall not exceed one for every thirty Thousand, but each State shall have at Least one Representative; and until such enumeration shall be made, the State of New Hampshire shall be entitled to chuse three, Massachusetts eight, Rhode-Island and Providence Plantations one, Connecticut five, New-York six, New Jersey four, Pennsylvania eight, Delaware one, Maryland six, Virginia ten, North Carolina five, South Carolina five, and Georgia three.

When vacancies happen in the Representation from any State, the Executive Authority thereof shall issue Writs of Election to fill such Vacancies.

The House of Representatives shall chuse their Speaker and other Officers; and shall have the sole Power of Impeachment.

Section. 3.
The Senate of the United States shall be composed of two Senators from each State, chosen by the Legislature thereof for six Years; and each Senator shall have one Vote.

Immediately after they shall be assembled in Consequence of the first Election, they shall be divided as equally as may be into three Classes. The Seats of the Senators of the first Class shall be vacated at the Expiration of the second Year, of the second Class at the Expiration of the fourth Year, and of the third Class at the Expiration of the sixth Year, so that one third may be chosen every second Year; and if Vacancies happen by Resignation, or otherwise, during the Recess of the Legislature of any State, the Executive thereof may make temporary Appointments until the next Meeting of the Legislature, which shall then fill such Vacancies.

No Person shall be a Senator who shall not have attained to the Age of thirty Years, and been nine Years a Citizen of the United States, and who shall not, when elected, be an Inhabitant of that State for which he shall be chosen.

The Vice-President of the United States shall be President of the Senate, but shall have no Vote, unless they be equally divided.

The Senate shall chuse their other Officers, and also a President pro tempore, in the Absence of the Vice President, or when he shall exercise the Office of President of the United States.

The Senate shall have the sole Power to try all Impeachments. When sitting for that Purpose, they shall be on Oath or Affirmation. When the President of the United States is tried, the Chief Justice shall preside: And no Person shall be convicted without the Concurrence of two thirds of the Members present.

Judgment in Cases of Impeachment shall not extend further than to removal from Office, and disqualification to hold and enjoy any Office of honor, Trust or Profit under the United States: but the Party convicted shall nevertheless be liable and subject to Indictment, Trial, Judgment and Punishment, according to Law.

Section. 4.

The Times, Places and Manner of holding Elections for Senators and Representatives, shall be prescribed in each State by the Legislature thereof; but the Congress may at any time by Law make or alter such Regulations, except as to the Places of chusing Senators.

The Congress shall assemble at least once in every Year, and such Meeting shall be on the first Monday in December, unless they shall by Law appoint a different Day.

Section. 5.

Each House shall be the Judge of the Elections, Returns and Qualifications of its own Members, and a Majority of each shall constitute a Quorum to do Business; but a smaller Number may adjourn from day to day, and may be authorized to compel the Attendance of absent Members, in such Manner, and under such Penalties as each House may provide.

Each House may determine the Rules of its Proceedings, punish its Members for disorderly Behaviour, and, with the Concurrence of two thirds, expel a Member.

Each House shall keep a Journal of its Proceedings, and from time to time publish the same, excepting such Parts as may in their Judgment require Secrecy; and the Yeas and Nays of the Members of either House on any question shall, at the Desire of one fifth of those Present, be entered on the Journal.

Neither House, during the Session of Congress, shall, without the Consent of the other, adjourn for more than three days, nor to any other Place than that in which the two Houses shall be sitting.

Section. 6.

The Senators and Representatives shall receive a Compensation for their Services, to be ascertained by Law, and paid out of the Treasury of the United States. They shall in all Cases, except Treason, Felony and Breach of the Peace, be privileged from Arrest during their Attendance at the Session of their respective Houses, and in going to and returning from the same; and for any Speech or Debate in either House, they shall not be questioned in any other Place.

No Senator or Representative shall, during the Time for which he was elected, be appointed to any civil Office under the Authority of the United States, which shall have been created, or the Emoluments whereof shall have been encreased during such time; and no Person holding any Office under the United States, shall be a Member of either House during his Continuance in Office.

Section. 7.

All Bills for raising Revenue shall originate in the House of Representatives; but the Senate may propose or concur with Amendments as on other Bills.

Every Bill which shall have passed the House of Representatives and the Senate, shall, before it become a Law, be presented to the President of the United States: If he approve he shall sign it, but if not he shall return it, with his Objections to that House in which it shall have originated, who shall enter the Objections at large on their Journal, and proceed to reconsider it. If after such Reconsideration two thirds of that House shall agree to pass the Bill, it shall be sent, together with the Objections, to the other House, by which it shall likewise be reconsidered, and if approved by two thirds of that House, it shall become a Law. But in all such Cases the Votes of both Houses shall be determined by yeas and Nays, and the Names of the Persons voting for and against the Bill shall be entered on the Journal of each House respectively. If any Bill shall not be returned by the President within ten Days (Sundays excepted) after it shall have been presented to him, the Same shall be a Law, in like Manner as if he had signed it, unless the Congress by their Adjournment prevent its Return, in which Case it shall not be a Law.

Every Order, Resolution, or Vote to which the Concurrence of the Senate and House of Representatives may be necessary (except on a question of Adjournment) shall be presented to the President of the United States; and before the Same shall take Effect, shall be approved by him, or being disapproved by him, shall be repassed by two thirds of the Senate and House of Representatives, according to the Rules and Limitations prescribed in the Case of a Bill.

Section. 8.
The Congress shall have Power To lay and collect Taxes, Duties, Imposts and Excises, to pay the Debts and provide for the common Defence and general Welfare of the United States; but

all Duties, Imposts and Excises shall be uniform throughout the United States;

To borrow Money on the credit of the United States;

To regulate Commerce with foreign Nations, and among the several States, and with the Indian Tribes;

To establish an uniform Rule of Naturalization, and uniform Laws on the subject of Bankruptcies throughout the United States;

To coin Money, regulate the Value thereof, and of foreign Coin, and fix the Standard of Weights and Measures;

To provide for the Punishment of counterfeiting the Securities and current Coin of the United States;

To establish Post Offices and post Roads;

To promote the Progress of Science and useful Arts, by securing for limited Times to Authors and Inventors the exclusive Right to their respective Writings and Discoveries;

To constitute Tribunals inferior to the supreme Court;

To define and punish Piracies and Felonies committed on the high Seas, and Offences against the Law of Nations;

To declare War, grant Letters of Marque and Reprisal, and make Rules concerning Captures on Land and Water;

To raise and support Armies, but no Appropriation of Money to that Use shall be for a longer Term than two Years;

To provide and maintain a Navy;

To make Rules for the Government and Regulation of the land and naval Forces;

To provide for calling forth the Militia to execute the Laws of the Union, suppress Insurrections and repel Invasions;

To provide for organizing, arming, and disciplining, the Militia, and for governing such Part of them as may be employed in the Service of the United States, reserving to the States respectively, the Appointment of the Officers, and the Authority of training the Militia according to the discipline prescribed by Congress;

To exercise exclusive Legislation in all Cases whatsoever, over such District (not exceeding ten Miles square) as may, by Cession of particular States, and the Acceptance of Congress, become the Seat of the Government of the United States, and to exercise like Authority over all Places purchased by the Consent of the Legislature of the State in which the Same shall be, for the Erection of Forts, Magazines, Arsenals, dock-Yards, and other needful Buildings;—And

To make all Laws which shall be necessary and proper for carrying into Execution the foregoing Powers, and all other Powers vested by this Constitution in the Government of the United States, or in any Department or Officer thereof.

Section. 9.

The Migration or Importation of such Persons as any of the States now existing shall think proper to admit, shall not be prohibited by the Congress prior to the Year one thousand eight hundred and eight, but a Tax or duty may be imposed on such Importation, not exceeding ten dollars for each Person.

The Privilege of the Writ of Habeas Corpus shall not be suspended, unless when in Cases of Rebellion or Invasion the public Safety may require it.

No Bill of Attainder or ex post facto Law shall be passed.

No Capitation, or other direct, Tax shall be laid, unless in Proportion to the Census or enumeration herein before directed to be taken.

No Tax or Duty shall be laid on Articles exported from any State.
No Preference shall be given by any Regulation of Commerce or Revenue to the Ports of one State over those of another; nor shall Vessels bound to, or from, one State, be obliged to enter, clear, or pay Duties in another.

No Money shall be drawn from the Treasury, but in Consequence of Appropriations made by Law; and a regular Statement and Account of the Receipts and Expenditures of all public Money shall be published from time to time.

No Title of Nobility shall be granted by the United States: And no Person holding any Office of Profit or Trust under them, shall, without the Consent of the Congress, accept of any present, Emolument, Office, or Title, of any kind whatever, from any King, Prince, or foreign State.

Section. 10.
No State shall enter into any Treaty, Alliance, or Confederation; grant Letters of Marque and Reprisal; coin Money; emit Bills of Credit; make any Thing but gold and silver Coin a Tender in Payment of Debts; pass any Bill of Attainder, ex post facto Law, or Law impairing the Obligation of Contracts, or grant any Title of Nobility.

No State shall, without the Consent of the Congress, lay any Imposts or Duties on Imports or Exports, except what may be absolutely necessary for executing its inspection Laws: and the net Produce of all Duties and Imposts, laid by any State on Imports or Exports, shall be for the Use of the Treasury of the United States; and all such Laws shall be subject to the Revision and Controul of the Congress.

No State shall, without the Consent of Congress, lay any Duty of Tonnage, keep Troops, or Ships of War in time of Peace, enter into any Agreement or Compact with another State, or with a foreign Power, or engage in War, unless actually invaded, or in such imminent Danger as will not admit of delay.

Article. II.

Section. 1.
The executive Power shall be vested in a President of the United States of America. He shall hold his Office during the Term of four Years, and, together with the Vice President, chosen for the same Term, be elected, as follows:

Each State shall appoint, in such Manner as the Legislature thereof may direct, a Number of Electors, equal to the whole Number of Senators and Representatives to which the State may be entitled in the Congress: but no Senator or Representative, or Person holding an Office of Trust or Profit under the United States, shall be appointed an Elector.

The Electors shall meet in their respective States, and vote by Ballot for two Persons, of whom one at least shall not be an Inhabitant of the same State with themselves. And they shall make a List of all the Persons voted for, and of the Number of Votes for each; which List they shall sign and certify, and transmit sealed to the Seat of the Government of the United States, directed to the President of the Senate. The President of the Senate shall, in the Presence of the Senate and House of Representatives, open all the Certificates, and the Votes shall then be counted. The Person having the greatest Number of Votes shall be the President, if such Number be a Majority of the whole Number of Electors appointed; and if there be more than one who have such Majority, and have an equal Number of Votes, then the House of Representatives shall immediately chuse by Ballot one of them for President; and if no Person have a Majority, then from the five highest on the List the said House shall in like Manner chuse the President. But in chusing the President, the Votes shall be taken by States, the Representation from each State having one Vote; A quorum for this purpose shall consist of a Member or Members from two thirds of the States, and a Majority of all the States shall be necessary to a Choice. In every Case, after the Choice of the President, the Person having the greatest Number of Votes of the Electors shall be the Vice President. But if there should remain two or more who have equal Votes, the Senate shall chuse from them by Ballot the Vice President.

The Congress may determine the Time of chusing the Electors, and the Day on which they shall give their Votes; which Day shall be the same throughout the United States.

No Person except a natural born Citizen, or a Citizen of the United States, at the time of the Adoption of this Constitution, shall be eligible to the Office of President; neither shall any Person be eligible to that Office who shall not have attained to the Age of thirty five Years, and been fourteen Years a Resident within the United States.

In Case of the Removal of the President from Office, or of his Death, Resignation, or Inability to discharge the Powers and Duties of the said Office, the Same shall devolve on the Vice President, and the Congress may by Law provide for the Case of Removal, Death, Resignation or Inability, both of the President and Vice President, declaring what Officer shall then act as President, and such Officer shall act accordingly, until the Disability be removed, or a President shall be elected.

The President shall, at stated Times, receive for his Services, a Compensation, which shall neither be increased nor diminished during the Period for which he shall have been elected, and he shall not receive within that Period any other Emolument from the United States, or any of them.

Before he enter on the Execution of his Office, he shall take the following Oath or Affirmation:—"I do solemnly swear (or affirm) that I will faithfully execute the Office of President of the United States, and will to the best of my Ability, preserve, protect and defend the Constitution of the United States."

Section. 2.

The President shall be Commander in Chief of the Army and Navy of the United States, and of the Militia of the several States, when called into the actual Service of the United States; he may require the Opinion, in writing, of the principal Officer in each of the executive Departments, upon any Subject relating to the Duties of their respective Offices, and he shall have Power to grant Reprieves and Pardons for Offences against the United States, except in Cases of Impeachment.

He shall have Power, by and with the Advice and Consent of the Senate, to make Treaties, provided two thirds of the Senators present concur; and he shall nominate, and by and with the Advice and Consent of the Senate, shall appoint Ambassadors, other public Ministers and Consuls, Judges of the supreme Court, and all other Officers of the United States, whose Appointments are not herein otherwise provided for, and which shall be established by Law: but the Congress may by Law vest the Appointment of such inferior Officers, as they think proper, in the President alone, in the Courts of Law, or in the Heads of Departments.

The President shall have Power to fill up all Vacancies that may happen during the Recess of the Senate, by granting Commissions which shall expire at the End of their next Session.

Section. 3.

He shall from time to time give to the Congress Information of the State of the Union, and recommend to their Consideration such Measures as he shall judge necessary and expedient; he may, on extraordinary Occasions, convene both Houses, or either of them, and in Case of Disagreement between them, with Respect to the Time of Adjournment, he may adjourn them to such Time as he shall think proper; he shall receive Ambassadors and other public Ministers; he shall take Care that the Laws be faithfully executed, and shall Commission all the Officers of the United States.

Section. 4.

The President, Vice President and all civil Officers of the United States, shall be removed from Office on Impeachment for, and Conviction of, Treason, Bribery, or other high Crimes and Misdemeanors.

Article III.

Section. 1.

The judicial Power of the United States shall be vested in one supreme Court, and in such inferior Courts as the Congress may from time to time ordain and establish. The Judges, both of the supreme and inferior Courts, shall hold their Offices during good Behaviour, and shall, at stated Times, receive for their Services a Compensation, which shall not be diminished during their Continuance in Office.

Section. 2.

The judicial Power shall extend to all Cases, in Law and Equity, arising under this Constitution, the Laws of the United States, and Treaties made, or which shall be made, under their Authority;—to all Cases affecting Ambassadors, other public Ministers and Consuls;--to all Cases of admiralty and maritime Jurisdiction;—to Controversies to which the United States shall be a Party;—to Controversies between two or more States;—between a State and Citizens of another State,—between Citizens of different States,—between Citizens of the same State claiming Lands under Grants of different States, and between a State, or the Citizens thereof, and foreign States, Citizens or Subjects.

In all Cases affecting Ambassadors, other public Ministers and Consuls, and those in which a State shall be Party, the supreme Court shall have original Jurisdiction. In all the other Cases before mentioned, the supreme Court shall have appellate Jurisdiction, both as to Law and Fact, with such Exceptions, and under such Regulations as the Congress shall make.

The Trial of all Crimes, except in Cases of Impeachment, shall be by Jury; and such Trial shall be held in the State where the said Crimes shall have been committed; but when not committed within any State, the Trial shall be at such Place or Places as the Congress may by Law have directed.

Section. 3.

Treason against the United States, shall consist only in levying War against them, or in adhering to their Enemies, giving them Aid and Comfort. No Person shall be convicted of Treason unless on the Testimony of two Witnesses to the same overt Act, or on Confession in open Court.

The Congress shall have Power to declare the Punishment of Treason, but no Attainder of Treason shall work Corruption of Blood, or Forfeiture except during the Life of the Person attainted.

Article. IV.

Section. 1.

Full Faith and Credit shall be given in each State to the public Acts, Records, and judicial Proceedings of every other State. And the Congress may by general Laws prescribe the Manner in which such Acts, Records and Proceedings shall be proved, and the Effect thereof.

Section. 2.

The Citizens of each State shall be entitled to all Privileges and Immunities of Citizens in the several States.

A Person charged in any State with Treason, Felony, or other Crime, who shall flee from Justice, and be found in another State, shall on Demand of the executive Authority of the State from which he fled, be delivered up, to be removed to the State having Jurisdiction of the Crime.

No Person held to Service or Labour in one State, under the Laws thereof, escaping into another, shall, in Consequence of any Law or Regulation therein, be discharged from such Service or Labour, but shall be delivered up on Claim of the Party to whom such Service or Labour may be due.

Section. 3.
New States may be admitted by the Congress into this Union; but no new State shall be formed or erected within the Jurisdiction of any other State; nor any State be formed by the Junction of two or more States, or Parts of States, without the Consent of the Legislatures of the States concerned as well as of the Congress.

The Congress shall have Power to dispose of and make all needful Rules and Regulations respecting the Territory or other Property belonging to the United States; and nothing in this Constitution shall be so construed as to Prejudice any Claims of the United States, or of any particular State.

Section. 4.
The United States shall guarantee to every State in this Union a Republican Form of Government, and shall protect each of them against Invasion; and on Application of the Legislature, or of the Executive (when the Legislature cannot be convened), against domestic Violence.

Article. V.

The Congress, whenever two thirds of both Houses shall deem it necessary, shall propose Amendments to this Constitution, or, on the Application of the Legislatures of two thirds of the several

States, shall call a Convention for proposing Amendments, which, in either Case, shall be valid to all Intents and Purposes, as Part of this Constitution, when ratified by the Legislatures of three fourths of the several States, or by Conventions in three fourths thereof, as the one or the other Mode of Ratification may be proposed by the Congress; Provided that no Amendment which may be made prior to the Year One thousand eight hundred and eight shall in any Manner affect the first and fourth Clauses in the Ninth Section of the first Article; and that no State, without its Consent, shall be deprived of its equal Suffrage in the Senate.

Article. VI.

All Debts contracted and Engagements entered into, before the Adoption of this Constitution, shall be as valid against the United States under this Constitution, as under the Confederation.

This Constitution, and the Laws of the United States which shall be made in Pursuance thereof; and all Treaties made, or which shall be made, under the Authority of the United States, shall be the supreme Law of the Land; and the Judges in every State shall be bound thereby, any Thing in the Constitution or Laws of any State to the Contrary notwithstanding.

The Senators and Representatives before mentioned, and the Members of the several State Legislatures, and all executive and judicial Officers, both of the United States and of the several States, shall be bound by Oath or Affirmation, to support this Constitution; but no religious Test shall ever be required as a Qualification to any Office or public Trust under the United States.

Article. VII.

The Ratification of the Conventions of nine States, shall be sufficient for the Establishment of this Constitution between the States so ratifying the Same.

The Word, "the," being interlined between the seventh and eighth Lines of the first Page, the Word "Thirty" being partly written on an Erazure in the fifteenth Line of the first Page, The Words "is tried" being interlined between the thirty second and thirty third Lines of the first Page and the Word "the" being interlined between the forty third and forty fourth Lines of the second Page.

Attest William Jackson Secretary

Done in Convention by the Unanimous Consent of the States present the Seventeenth Day of September in the Year of our Lord one thousand seven hundred and Eighty seven and of the Independence of the United States of America the Twelfth In witness whereof We have hereunto subscribed our Names

The Bill of Rights

Amendment I
Congress shall make no law respecting an establishment of religion, or prohibiting the free exercise thereof; or abridging the freedom of speech, or of the press; or the right of the people peaceably to assemble, and to petition the government for a redress of grievances.

Amendment II
A well regulated militia, being necessary to the security of a free state, the right of the people to keep and bear arms, shall not be infringed.

Amendment III
No soldier shall, in time of peace be quartered in any house, without the consent of the owner, nor in time of war, but in a manner to be prescribed by law.

Amendment   IV
The right of the people to be secure in their persons, houses, papers, and effects, against unreasonable searches and seizures, shall not be violated, and no warrants shall issue, but upon probable cause, supported by oath or affirmation, and particularly describing the place to be searched, and the persons or things to be seized.

Amendment V
No person shall be held to answer for a capital, or otherwise infamous crime, unless on a presentment or indictment of a grand jury, except in cases arising in the land or naval forces, or

in the militia, when in actual service in time of war or public danger; nor shall any person be subject for the same offense to be twice put in jeopardy of life or limb; nor shall be compelled in any criminal case to be a witness against himself, nor be deprived of life, liberty, or property, without due process of law; nor shall private property be taken for public use, without just compensation.

Amendment VI
In all criminal prosecutions, the accused shall enjoy the right to a speedy and public trial, by an impartial jury of the state and district wherein the crime shall have been committed, which district shall have been previously ascertained by law, and to be informed of the nature and cause of the accusation; to be confronted with the witnesses against him; to have compulsory process for obtaining witnesses in his favor, and to have the assistance of counsel for his defense.

Amendment VIIn suits at common law, where the value in controversy shall exceed twenty dollars, the right of trial by jury shall be preserved, and no fact tried by a jury, shall be otherwise reexamined in any court of the United States, than according to the rules of the common law.

Amendment VIII
Excessive bail shall not be required, nor excessive fines imposed, nor cruel and unusual punishments inflicted.

Amendment IX

The enumeration in the Constitution, of certain rights, shall not be construed to deny or disparage others retained by the people.

Amendment X

The powers not delegated to the United States by the Constitution, nor prohibited by it to the states, are reserved to the states respectively, or to the people.

References

Allison, Andrew. *The Real Thomas Jefferson*. National Center for Constitutional Studies, 1983.

Anderson, Jack and Daryl Gibson. *Peace, War, and Politics: An Eyewitness Account*. Forge Books, 1999.

Baron, Robert (ed.). *Thomas Jefferson the Man: In His Own Words*. Fulcrum Publishing, 1996.

Bernstein, R.B. *Thomas Jefferson*. Oxford University Press, 2005.

Bork, Robert. *Slouching Towards Gomorrah: Modern Liberalism and American Decline*. HarperCollins, 1996.

Coulter, Ann. *High Crimes and Misdemeanors: The Case Against Bill Clinton*. Regnery, 2002.

Diggins, John. *Ronald Reagan*. WW Norton, 2008.

Ellis, Joseph. *American Sphinx: The Character of Thomas Jefferson*. Vintage, 1998.

Ellis, Joseph. *Founding Brothers: The Revolutionary Generation*. Vintage, 2002.

Ferris, Jeri. *Thomas Jefferson, Father of Liberty.* Carolrhoda Books, 1998.

Flexner, Thomas. *Washington: The Indispensible Man.* Back Bay Books, 1994.

Franklin, Benjamin. *The Autobiography of Ben Franklin.* Greenbook Publications, 2010.

Gibson, John. *The War on Christmas: How the Liberal Plot to Ban the Sacred Christian Holiday Is Worse Than You Thought.* Sentinel Trade, 2006.

Gilbert, Martin. *Churchill: A Life.* Holt, 1992.

Gingrich, Newt. *Real Change from the World That Fails to the World That Works.* Tantor Media, 2008.

Irving, Washington. *Life of George Washington.* General Books, 2009.

Levin, Mark. *Liberty and Tyranny.* Threshold Editions, 2009.

Marton, Kati. *The Polk Conspiracy.* Three Rivers Press, 1992.

McCullough, David. *1776.* Simon & Schuster, 2005.

Morris, Dick. *Fleeced.* HarperCollins, 2008.

Noonan, Peggy. *When Character Was King: A Story of Ronald Reagan.* Viking, 2001.

Paine, Thomas. *Common Sense.* CreateSpace, 2010.

Skousen, W. Cleon. *The 5000 Year Leap.* National Center for Constitutional Studies, 1981.

Skousen, W. Cleon. *The Making of America: The Substance and Meaning of the Constitution.* National Center for Constitutional Studies, 1985.

Sowell, Thomas. *Black Rednecks and White Liberals.* Encounter Books, 2005.

Stewart, Chris, and Ted Stewart. *Seven Miracles That Saved America.* Shadow Mountain, 2009.

Steyn, Mark. *America Alone: The End of the World As We Know It.* Regnery Press, 2006.

Stossel, John. *Myths, Lies and Downright Stupidity.* Hyperion, 2006.

Acknowledgments

I would like to thank my wife, Diana, for all of her love and support. She has been my guiding light in life as well supporting me in writing this book. I don't know if I would have written this book without her unwavering support and patience. She loves this country as I do and believes that without people like Thomas Jefferson and the other Founding Fathers, America would not only be a different place but most likely there would not have been an America.

I would also like to thank Jim Long who is a retired teacher who showed real excitement when I discussed the writing of the book with him. He was the first person to read the manuscript. He believed as I do that, if we are to survive as a free nation, we must look back to the Constitution for guidance.

I most want to thank the writers of the books that I have read on this subject, especially *The Making of America, The 5000 Year Leap, The Real Thomas Jefferson,* and *American Sphinx: The Character of Thomas Jefferson.* I highly recommend the reading of these important books as they will give you further insight into how this great nation was formed and the individuals who were instrumental in its creation.

About the Author

Steve Hanson

Steve Hanson grew up in the Midwest with traditional family values. His Army service in Vietnam dramatically changed his views on life and enhanced his love of country. His lifelong work in the financial field has given him a better understanding of the role of the federal government. Only exceeding his love of country is his love of God and family.

Hanson is a small business owner and mortgage loan executive. He and his wife, Diana, and their five children live in Omaha.